Why I Am a Priest

WHY
I Am a
PRIEST

THIRTY Success STORIES

Edited by
Lawrence Boadt, C.S.P.
and
Michael J. Hunt, C.S.P.

PAULIST PRESS
New York / Mahwah, N.J.

Acknowledgments
The Publisher gratefully acknowledges use of the following: Articles that originally appeared in *Emmanuel* magazine in recent years as part of the "Why I Am a Priest Today" series. Used with permission of Father Anthony Schueller, S.S.S., editor and publisher of *Emmanuel*. Excerpts from the English translation of the *Catechism of the Catholic Church* for the United States of America © 1994, United States Catholic Conference, Inc.—Libreria Editrice Vaticana. Used with permission.

Cover design by Lynn Else and Valerie Petro

Cover photo by Gene Plaisted

Copyright © 1999 by Paulist Press, Inc.

Library of Congress Cataloging-in-Publication Data

Why I am a priest : thirty success stories / [compiled by] Lawrence Boadt and Michael Hunt.
    p. cm.
  ISBN 0-8091-3910-3 (alk. paper)
    1. Catholic Church—Clergy—Biography. I. Boadt, Lawrence. II. Hunt, Michael J., 1941-
BX4651.2.W49 1999
262'.142—dc21

                                     99-048306
                                         CIP

Published by Paulist Press
997 Macarthur Boulevard
Mahwah, New Jersey 07430

www.paulistpress.com

Printed and bound in the
United States of America

CONTENTS

INTRODUCTION

by Lawrence Boadt, C.S.P.
Publisher, Paulist Press

I.

There seems to be no question more hotly debated among Catholics than "What is happening to priests and the priesthood today?" It is has become the topic of debates on the national news and of sensational features about priests who have failed in their personal lives or their pastoral responsibilities. It has generated agonized soul-searching over the declining numbers of priests and a growing dismay over the shortage of vocations because of the inevitable long-term effects this will have on keeping parishes alive. Not to mention that in many quarters, there is the heated anger generated by the subject of ordaining women to the priesthood.

One of the great dangers from an unrelenting diet of these issues for the church as a community of followers of Jesus Christ is that the true spiritual center and daily work of being church becomes obscured and neglected in our awareness by concentrating on such mainly organizational aspects that feed into journalistic interests of conflict and controversy. We begin to visualize being Catholic as being part of a social phenomenon revealed largely in media events, rather than as being *primarily* the action of God and a life of grace.

No piece of the church's identity has suffered more in this shift of focus from spirituality to sociology than the role of the priesthood. Perhaps the word *role* is not quite adequate. Surely many roles and tasks that priests perform have changed dramatically as Catholic populations swell and modern ideas and technologies change in our society, but the heart of the matter is really the spiritual "life" of the priesthood, not its roles. In the ever mounting discussion about the priest today, the spiritual dimension is often forgotten. And yet I cannot think of a single one of my fellow priests whom I have met in frequent travels all over the United States and Canada who did not see his commitment first and foremost as service to God's people, together with personal growth as a servant of Christ in his own life. As imperfectly as they may later embody either or both of these ideals, they did choose them with an open and generous heart when they became priests. It is imperative that we do not forget this vital quality of what being a priest really means to the one who exercises it—and to the church as a community of faith, hope and love of God.

Cardinal Joseph Bernardin, before he died, spoke to his fellow priests of this struggle to understand the proper role of the priest:

> There is a curious tension today in regard to the priesthood. On the one hand, there is a great deal of hand wringing and anguish over the identity and role of priests as well as their diminishing numbers, and on the other hand, our culture is crying out for what I have called mystagogues or bearers of the mystery of God and doctors of the soul. I suggest that this tension or dilemma could be resolved if we realize that what our people so desperately need is precisely what we priests are uniquely equipped to provide: nourishment for the soul.
>
> We are not indispensable "functionaries" in the church; we are bridges to the very mystery of God and healers of the soul. When we claim this identity unapologetically, we not only find ourselves; we also provide the church and our culture with the sustenance they require.

This is the vocation, the reality, to which we are called. It is not dependent on numbers, or structures, or chancery offices, or any of the things we thought so essential, so important but now are completely changed or are no more. Rather, it is dependent on the Lord Jesus (who is the mystery of God and the healer of the soul) whom we make present in a tangible and inviting way each day to the countless people whom we serve. ("Priests, Religious Leaders, Doctors of the Soul" [*Origins*, May 25, 1995], 27–28)

II.

This short book gathers the witness of a wide variety of priests who are able to share with the reader their insights into being a priest, their identities, their awareness of weakness, their hopes and dreams. Because they write about themselves, their stories reveal that some very ordinary but dedicated people can find a way both to follow Christ in the present difficult age and bring an awareness of his love to others.

Pope John Paul II has likened the commitment of a priest to the people of God to that of a married couple to each other. The priest, he writes, "will always remain a member of the community as a believer alongside his other brothers and sisters...but in virtue of his configuration to Christ...the priest stands in a spousal relationship with regard to the community" (1992 encyclical letter, *Pastores dabo Vobis*). A priest gives his life and his ability to love as a commitment to the church as a human community with the same depth of devotion that a husband and a wife give to each other.

The *Catechism of the Catholic Church* expresses this commitment to the community of the church that a priest seeks to make real in his own life in another way:

> Intrinsically linked to the sacramental nature of ecclesial ministry is *its character as service*. Entirely dependent on Christ who gives mission and authority, ministers are truly "slaves of Christ" (cf. Rom 1:1), in the image of him who

freely took "the form of a slave" for us (Phil 2:7). Because
the word and grace of which they are ministers are not their
own, but are given to them by Christ for the sake of others,
they must freely become the slaves of all (cf. 1 Cor 9:19).
(par. 876)

III.

Perhaps no aspect of the priesthood is so under question and
in need of priests' own testimony than why they are willing to
undertake the life of celibacy for the service of the church. While
not producing a "tell-all" tabloid story about the daily struggles of
their sexuality, the priests in this volume clearly reveal how their
decision for celibacy influences and animates their priesthood. If
I had to find a way to capture what that celibacy means for these
priests from the combined total of the many small vignettes scat-
tered throughout their stories, it might be similar to the way the
well-known author Kathleen Norris reflects on it in her best-
selling work, *Cloister Walk* (New York: Riverhead Books, 1996;
pages 116–21), as described by Father Thomas Rausch in his own
very worthwhile reflection on the contemporary notion of priesthood:

> A celibacy that works is one practiced by people who are
> fully aware of their sexuality but able to express it in a celi-
> bate way; it means accepting sublimation as a normal part of
> adulthood. The fruit of such a healthy celibacy is hospitality
> and a gift for friendship with all people, men and women,
> old and young. ("Priesthood in the Church of Tomorrow,"
> *Origins* 27 [November 13, 1997], 374)

IV.

Finally, no priest in these stories or elsewhere claims that his
priestly vocation has ever made him perfect nor even that it has
helped him to be a more spiritually mature person than anyone

else. A spirit of humble awareness of a priest's faults and limitations, his capacity for evil as great as anyone's, is a true thread among these essays. Once again, the *Catechism of the Catholic Church* says it well when it notes:

> This presence of Christ in the minister is not to be understood as if the latter were preserved from all human weaknesses, the spirit of domination, error, even sin. The power of the Holy Spirit does not guarantee all acts of ministers in the same way. While this guarantee extends to the sacraments, so that even the minister's sin cannot impede the fruit of grace, in many other acts the minister leaves human traces that are not always signs of fidelity to the Gospel and consequently can harm the apostolic fruitfulness of the Church. (par. 1550)

V.

Ultimately, priesthood is not so much a *work* for the church, as a *life* in and of the church. Or to put it more ultimately yet, it is each individual priest living a relationship to Christ, first as a disciple, and then as a friend; to the church, first as a servant, and then as a spouse; to the people of God, first as a leader, but as much a colleague and fellow pilgrim; to the world, first as a mortal bit of its matter, but as much the singer of its glory to raise its joyful song of hope for all to hear.

Reflecting on being a priest today, Father Robert Rausch has suggested that a distinctive priestly spirituality should encompass four qualities: *prayerfulness, leadership, participation* and *service*. I believe that you will discover that this description is well borne out in the following personal reflections by thirty fully contemporary and fully dedicated priests.

May their stories encourage many other young men to hear the call of Christ to a priestly vocation!

ANTHONY M. PILLA

As I begin this presidential address, I would like to join our episcopal conference in thanking God for the great gift to our church, the priesthood of Pope John Paul II.

He chose priesthood at a time and place where such a choice was dangerous and, in the eyes of many at that time, foolhardy. Since that moment he has always and everywhere courageously manifested the heart of a priest.

Since becoming our Holy Father, he has continued to be a true priest.

It is in the celebration of the Eucharist that this Holy Father has revealed the special intensity of his commitment to his vocation. Whether seen by millions on television among the splendor which is St. Peter's or seen only by those in his immediate congregation in the privacy of his chapel, Pope John Paul enters as intimately and profoundly into the mystery of Christ's redemptive act as any priest ever has.

But beyond the purely ceremonial, his priesthood is also revealed in the compassion that has led him to travel the world to speak and act tirelessly on behalf of humanity in need. And who can forget that special trip to the Rome prison to forgive his would-be assassin?

From a World Day of Peace in Assisi to a World Day of Youth in Denver, and many points in between, the Holy Father has mobilized the power of faith and the power of prayer in a way that surely prevailed on God's loving providence to replace the fear that humanity has been living under for its very future with a new hope...

My brother bishops, in accord with the ministry of this *sacerdos magnus*, this great "high priest," I wish to speak to you today of all our priests and their special service to the church.

Like many of you, it has been my experience, as a priest and as a bishop, that our people not only greatly admire and love our Holy Father but they also love their priests, and so do we. Our people are kind and gracious to us to a fault, often forgiving us when perhaps challenging us would be more to our benefit.

It is also my experience that our priests love their people. It is their regular joy to share the privileged moments of their people's lives, whether in sorrow or joy, and to relate these moments to God's providential love. Sometimes we forget that it is not easy to share times of sorrow. Words, which other times come so easily to our lips, often fail us in the presence of those who have lost a loved one or who themselves are facing suffering without quite knowing why God is asking them to do so. Yet, it is precisely in these moments that the priest is there, with his own words of personal faith and with his compassionate presence.

We should not forget that even times of joy can bring their own challenges: celebrating baptisms Sunday after Sunday for large numbers of children; offering four Masses on a Saturday, including the daily Mass, a funeral, a wedding, and the vigil Mass; presiding at five first communion ceremonies in May of every year. These are not uncommon experiences for our priests today.

In joy and sorrow, our priests find in their people the reason they chose to be priests in the first place, and we hope that our people find us to be loving witnesses, too, and a help in being true to our common faith.

My message to our priests today is one of support, of confidence in them, of respect for them in their ministry, and of the love that gathers us together in its binding force. So many negative images of priests are carelessly, even heartlessly spread around that today I believe it is both a duty and a joy to speak words of affirmation and reaffirmation for our priests.

We should not forget that we also share with our fellow priests the burdens and challenges of our times. Those of us who have lived through the last 30 years have experienced a period characterized by bounding hope and much fear mixed together. In the exciting days of the Second Vatican Council itself, perhaps we were innocent enough to think that renewal would be only full of hope and not at all disorienting. We were forgetful of the freedom of the Spirit who, blowing where the Spirit wills, sometimes blows things down.

As president of the National Council of Catholic Bishops, I have had the opportunity to talk to priests across our country. They do not expect miracles to come from words, or magical solutions to come from even our episcopal conference, but they do wish us to know that we show our respect for them when we bishops share with them, along with our hopes, our fears as well. I wish to address three fears which I think priests have, with the fervent prayer that in doing so I may contribute something to seeing that they do not become paralyzing fears, self-fulfilling prophecies, or ultimately overcome our priests and the church. The three things I wish to address are: the shortage of priests, the challenge of priestly leadership, and priestly life in general.

The Shortage of Priests

Our priests are worried about the shortage of priests and "graying" of the priestly fraternity. They worry about a "slow fadeout" for the priesthood, at least as we have known it. Growing out of this worry, the priests experience inner turmoil as they struggle to maintain a level of service to the people that their own sense of duty demands; they experience physical exhaustion brought on by fewer and older priests trying to do what more and younger priests once did; and, for some, there is an experience of a corrosive psychological temptation to question the relevance of a vocation that no longer seems to attract as many as it once did.

Although they have decreased greatly, departures from the priesthood of fellow priests, some of them dear friends, have also affected attitudes of both priests and people toward the priesthood and its permanent commitment.

Without vocations to support the magnificent structure of worship, education, and charitable service the church in this country has built, priests can experience a weariness of spirit. They find their personal resources are stretched to the limit by such necessities as one priest sometimes caring for more than one parish.

Against this backdrop, God is surely calling us to foster vocations with an intense awareness of what a treasure each vocation is. If once we reflected little on the contribution each member of the church can make to God's call being heard by those God seeks out, now we are urging people actively to take up the task of finding new workers to come to the harvest. I hope the priests of our nation understand that this is the purpose of our new vocation strategy, "A Future Full of Hope." Undoubtedly, such efforts will ultimately make the bond between our priests and people even closer as together we search out new priestly leaders.

Leadership

A second area affecting our priests today is what I choose to call "leadership concerns." The role of the priest in leading the Christian community has become ambiguous for many priests. The call of Vatican Council II for the renewal of the laity, to which many have so eagerly responded, has sometimes been treated like a "zero-sum" game, that is to say, the lay role increases only at the expense of the priest's role decreasing.

However, it is the priest to whom people turn to affirm them in their renewed roles. Consequently, a priest may sometimes feel as if there is less room for him in the church; at the same time he faces criticism if "Father" is not always present to respond to the many demands of leadership; and very capable parish priests often find that the "generalist" is no longer as well respected in the age of the "specialist."

Presiding at the Eucharist is a good example of the new demands that priests face as a result of the conciliar renewal. The roots of liturgical reform went back many decades before the council, but few of us fully understood what a challenge the reformed liturgy would be. The new order demands that the priest be a good celebrant and presider, an excellent preacher and exponent of God's word, a man of prayer able to lead others to pray, someone comfortable with sharing the liturgical roles that were once his alone. When a priest is unable to fulfill these varied demands, the liturgy then seems bereft of an essential element in its power to touch people and to lift their minds and hearts to God.

What I have just said of priests is also true of us bishops. Most of us were not trained to be leaders who are collaborative and authoritative because in former times there was little need to do so. Most of us also are still in the early stages of learning how best to respond to people's spiritual hunger through an experience of liturgy in which they are now active participants.

The ambiguities also affect the relationship between priests and bishops. Following the call of the council, we have often reaffirmed the closeness of the relationship. As the *Decree on the Bishops' Pastoral Office in the Church* says: "A bishop should always welcome priests with a special love since they assume in part the bishop's duties and cares and carry the weight of them day by day so zealously. He should regard his priests as sons and friends. Thus, by his readiness to listen to them and by his trusting familiarity, a bishop can work to promote the whole pastoral work of the entire diocese" (n.16c). The same document also urges: "For the sake of greater service to souls, let the bishop engage in discussion with his priests, even collectively, especially about pastoral matters. This he should do not only occasionally but, as far as possible. At fixed intervals" (n. 28).

As an episcopal conference, we have in the years since the council taken this call seriously, and have established the means that are leading, through good and bad experiences and difficult ones, to this kind of ministry of bishop and priest together. Yet, on the way there, I have heard from some priests that, while we bishops call our priests our closest collaborators, they too often feel themselves to be our most taken-for-granted employees.

We need to take the counsel of one another to come to reasonable expectations. We bishops should ask ourselves about the extent to which we truly empower our priests in their ministry, especially our pastors who so directly share in our role as shepherds of the flock. Priests, in turn, should ask themselves about the extent to which they truly empower us bishops as their leaders through their support and assistance. We share the stresses of administration, and this can and should be a source of unity and understanding among us.

The polarization within the church today is also a factor of parish life. We may think sometimes that we are on the front lines of these debates, but we take second place to our parish priests who deal with them daily.

Twenty-one years ago, a member of this conference from my state described the average pastor as being at the bottom of a huge funnel out of which poured onto his shoulders all the programs created by the Holy See, our episcopal conferences, national and state, and our own diocesan curias. The description is still valid, and gives birth to two questions: Do we empower our priests in their pastoral ministry, or do we burden them, stifling them with myriad programs and directives? Second, do we tell them they are our closest collaborators and then place a level of bureaucracy between them and us?

The challenges of the last 30 years, which I have described, have managed also to unleash a lot of creative energy. Bishops and priests together rejoice in the growing role of the laity, and we affirm our belief that a church made up of active priests, laity, and religious is a church better equipped to fulfill the Lord's vocation which he handed to us: to bring glad tidings to the poor and to all people. The questions to which I have given voice, involving the increased role of the laity in general, are also have the good effect of focusing more clearly on who the priest is and what his essential role is as one who forms community around word and sacrament.

Priestly Life

My third and final group of issues relates to priestly life. Once, large ordination classes of young men close to one another in age and experience, and also parishes staffed with several priests in urban areas offered natural opportunities for mutual spiritual and psychological support. Now these support systems generally are no longer in place.

Professional development is an area to which little attention was given in the past. Now, with the age of the "specialist" and the large number of religious and laity who have developed skills in areas such as religious education, liturgy, and social service, it is more imperative for priests to have the opportunity to both update skills that make them effective "generalists" and also to pursue particular skills and interests of importance to their ministry.

As bishops, we have encouraged programs and services to meet this need. But there is a need not only to offer them programs but also to offer them ourselves, as their fathers, brothers, and friends. We must show them that we, too, are lifelong learners. We need to offer them a broad rainbow of experiences in their ministry and avoid the easy temptation to fill vacant slots with warm bodies.

Priestly celibacy is a concern today. The attention placed on it in our time makes it a stress factor rather than a gift for the kingdom. There is little attempt by the media or others to understand the witness of celibacy, and its special charism often takes second place to a malicious pleasure at instances of its violation.

Sadly, some of our priests must share the blame for this. The painful last few years of instances of inappropriate behavior by a few have called into question the very notion of celibacy itself. While most of our people do not judge the priesthood by the behavior of an individual priest, and while they still have confidence in the vast majority of priests who serve them daily, one would not believe this to be true if one only heeded the written or electronic reports.

Without minimizing the harm done by these same few, I want to offer some pointed words to the condescending and derisive portrayals of priestly celibacy we often see.

In this time and in this nation, where the church not only does not suffer persecution and deprivation but even holds a place of prestige and influence, the priest's celibate commitment witnesses to the spirit of sacrifice that is essential to Christianity, to taking up one's cross daily in imitation of Christ, and to losing oneself in order to find oneself. To sacrifice marriage and a family of one's own is particularly relevant to our age in which sexuality is taken for granted and often debased. Celibacy in our times is a "sign of contradiction," and I salute the overwhelming majority of the priests of this nation who loyally and faithfully fulfill their promise of celibate chastity.

As scripture says, there is no greater love than to lay down one's life for one's friends. There is no greater sign of hope in the Lord than to believe that serving him is worth sacrificing the most truly human of all joys—marriage and family. It is also a sign of confidence in the church community for [its] priests to deprive themselves of the ordinary consolation of wife and children. Most people hope it is this consolation that will comfort them in their final years and ward off the loneliness that all fear will accompany old age. The priest forgoes this consolation, trusting that the community of the church will be his family and that it is not in vain to cast one's cares upon the Lord…I can think of no greater witness to their faith and to their sacrificial love for their sisters and brothers than the celibacy of priests and vowed religious!

Conclusion

While I have raised these very real concerns of our priests today, and the list is not complete by any means, the grace of God is manifest in the clear evidence that priests continue to find their vocation personally enriching and vital to the life of the church. Three years ago, one of the nation's influential newspapers did a survey of priests and religious around the world. The survey format itself aroused concern that it was based on the assumption—maybe even the hope—that a popular media image of priests and religious as demoralized, unhappy, and even mostly at odds with church teaching would be confirmed. The results were vastly different from those expectations and made it clear that, by an overwhelming majority, priests are dedicated to the priesthood and the church. As the newspaper's own report put it, with regard to priests and religious, "loyalty to the church as an institution is high among both groups and contrary to popular perceptions; so is their morale."

Let me now close with words from Paul's letter to the Christians at Philippi, which I think express our feeling for our priests and our prayer for them:

> I give thanks to my God each time I remember you. Always, in every prayer of mine for all of you, I make my prayer with joy, so full a part have you taken in the work of the Gospel from the day it first reached you till now. Of this I am certain, that he who began the good work in you will bring it to completion, ready for the day when Jesus Christ comes…May you reap through Jesus Christ the full harvest of your justification to God's glory and praise. (Phil 1:3–11)

GEORGE G. HIGGINS

I have never thought of being anything but a priest. I grew up in a solid Catholic family in St. Francis Xavier Parish in La Grange, Illinois, in a suburb southwest of the city, and attended its parish school. The pastor of the parish quietly encouraged me to attend Chicago's Quigley Preparatory Seminary (thankfully a day school) and personally took me to Quigley on the near north side of Chicago to enroll me as a student in the Class of 1929. After five years at Quigley, I moved to the archdiocesan major seminary, St. Mary of the Lake, forty miles northwest of the city. Ordained there in 1940, I fully expected to be assigned as an associate pastor ("curate" in those days), but instead I was assigned to do graduate studies in labor economics at the Catholic University of America in Washington, D.C.

After taking my degree at Catholic University in 1944, I expected to be assigned to the faculty at the major seminary in Mundelein, Illinois, with a part-time assignment as an associate pastor, but, again, Providence had other plans for me.

A fellow Chicago priest, Msgr. John Hayes, who is still going strong at the age of ninety, had been serving as Assistant Director of the Social Action Department of the Old National Catholic Welfare Conference, now the United States Catholic Conference. In the spring of 1944, just as I was completing my work at Catholic University, he became ill and had to take extended sick leave. I was asked to fill in for him during the summer of 1944, but, as things worked out, I remained at the conference for 36 years until my mandatory retirement from the staff at the age of 65.

During my 36 years at the conference (and my busy years of retirement, with residence at Catholic University) I was never involved directly in parish work, except part-time in the summer and for seven years as a resident at a parish in Washington, D.C. As a social action "bureaucrat," I carried on my atypical pastoral work half-time in Washington and the other half traveling throughout the United States and to some extent in Europe and Latin America. At the time of Vatican II, and for the two years of the preparatory stage of the council, I traveled back and forth to Rome repeatedly as a consultant to the council.

Given my lack of pastoral experience in the traditional sense of the word, I think it would be presumptuous on my part to write about the distinctive role of a diocesan priest in today's world. Instead, I propose to offer random reflections of a general nature of what the church was like, what the priesthood was like, and what our ministerial expectations were like sixty years ago. I scoured my library looking for helpful leads in this regard. The late Karl Rahner, among others, came to my rescue. Rahner repeatedly reminded us in his voluminous writings, that far-reaching changes of the most surprising kind have occurred since the Second Vatican Council, and he tried, perhaps more successfully than any of his fellow theologians, to help us come to terms with these unexpected and, for some, traumatically unsettling changes.

"How little," Rahner says, did we older people and ministers who grew up in the pre-Vatican II monolithic church "expect a church of the kind we have today." But what kind of church did we experience in the forties and fifties, and what is different about the church of today? Parenthetically I am grateful, because of the sense of historical perspective it has given me, that my priesthood has been chronologically split down the middle—twenty-five years before and twenty-five-odd years after the council. Be that as it may, all of us who have known the church before and after the council will presumably answer these questions in different ways or at least with different shades of emphasis. In any event, I suspect that Rahner's answer will resonate with many of us. During the century preceding Vatican II, as Rahner notes, "The church was the object of an almost fanatical love, regarded as our natural home, sustaining and sheltering us in our spirituality, where whatever we needed was available as a matter of course and had only to be willingly and joyfully appropriated. The church supported us; it did not need to be supported by us."

Rahner goes on to say, however:

> Today all this is different. We do not see the church so much as the *signum elevatum in nationes* ("the sign raised up before the nations"), as it was acclaimed at the First Vatican Council. What we now see is the poor church of sinners, the tent of the pilgrim people of God, pitched in the desert and shaken by all the storms of history, the church laboriously seeking its way into the future, groping and suffering many internal afflictions, striving over and over again to make sure of its faith; we are aware of a church of internal tensions and conflicts, we feel burdened in the church both by the reactionary callousness of the institutional factor and by the reckless modernism of some that threatens to squander the sacred heritage of faith and to destroy the memory of its historical experience.

For those who find it difficult to cope with this very sudden and totally unexpected change or series of changes in our personal and communal understanding of the church, perhaps the biblically grounded counsel of one of my former colleagues at Catholic University, the Jesuit scholar, Fr. Ladislaus Orsy, may help to ease their pain. "Insecurity and obscurity," Orsy reminds us in one of his earlier books, "are part of our human and Christian condition. We have to live with them. Let us pray the Lord, therefore, that he should not take them away. Let us pray rather for the face of confidence when we walk in the jungle or when we sail on the high seas....We do not trust in order, but in the Spirit who leads God's pilgrims through all the confusion."

Rahner would have agreed with Orsy. If the church appears to be confused today, Rahner wrote in 1977, it is because society is confused. Both go together. "Sometimes," he added, "I ask myself if, from the point of view of faith, this is all so bad. Why should we Christians and the church in an age of confusion have answers for everything instead of putting up with the confusion among our contemporaries? I believe that we must perhaps prepare ourselves for the fact that future history will appear grayer and more confused and will have less room for great and clear intellectual vision."

Rahner is right on target when he says that today's confusion is not all that bad. To the contrary, it may prove to be a providential blessing if it forces all of us, and the people we are privileged to serve, to develop a spirit of authentic Christian maturity, a deeper poverty of spirit, and a more profound spirit of Christian hope.

The poet Wordsworth wrote in the immediate aftermath of the French Revolution of 1789, "Bliss was it in that dawn to be alive. But to be young was very heaven." In retrospect, with all that we know about the savagery of the French Revolution, the poet's optimism sounds overly romantic, even naive, an exercise in undisciplined poetic license. All things considered, however, there is something to be said for the poet's spirit of optimism. As St. Augustine cautions us (Liturgy of the Hours for the Wednesday of the twentieth week in Ordinary Time), it makes no sense to be pining for the past. He cautioned his contemporaries:

> So we must not grumble, for as the Apostle says: "Some of them murmured and were destroyed by serpents." Is there any affliction now endured by mankind that was not endured by our fathers before us? What sufferings of ours even bear comparison with what we know of their sufferings? And yet you hear people complaining about this present day and age because things were so much better in former times. I wonder what would happen if they could be taken back to the days of their ancestors—would we not still

hear them complaining? You may think past ages were good, but it is only because you are not living in them.

Have we forgotten the flood and the calamitous times of famine and war whose history has been recorded precisely in order to keep us from complaining to God on account of our own time? Just think what those past ages were like. Is there any one of us who does not shudder to hear or read of them? Far from justifying complaints about our own time, they teach us how much we have to be thankful for.

Let me conclude these random ruminations about the past, the present, and the future with a few simple maxims:

1. Christian maturity is the one quality—perhaps more than all others—that will be required of all of us in the predictably troubled days that lie ahead. The capacity to choose among alternatives, but without conflicts, without anxieties, is a sign of Christian maturity and Christian freedom. As I have already suggested, the church is living in an era of unpredictable transition at all levels of its pastoral life. At times it will all seem very ambiguous. Those who do not have a sense of personal fulfillment ought not to blame the church but rather their lack of freedom and maturity that does not allow them to put up with ambiguous situations. The crises in our lives are the conditions that makes us free and mature.

2. In the future it will be impossible to be an authentic Christian without being a contemplative—in our case, not like the Desert Fathers of long ago but as mature Christians who have a personal experience of God and are capable of meeting God in history, in politics, in our brothers and sisters, and most fully through prayer. In this sense, Christian contemplation will guarantee the survival of faith in a secularized world of the future. St. Teresa of Avila tells us that no temptation that the Christian will ever face is more serious than that of giving up on prayer. That's as true today as it was in the equally troubled sixteenth century.

3. The role of women in the church and society is and will continue to be one of the greatest challenges facing us. To say that my generation was slow in facing up to this challenge would be a gross understatement. Coming generations must do better than we have done, "for the praise and glory of [God], for our good, and for the good of all his church," as we say at Mass each day, asking that our sacrifice may be acceptable to God.

4. We will also be expected to show greater leadership in promoting Christian unity and Catholic-Jewish understanding than our generation was able to do, at least until the Second Vatican Council.

5. One last word, which I hope will not sound patronizing or paternalistic. A recent scholarly study of American seminaries found, among other things, that the seminarian of today is less oriented toward social justice than his counterparts of a few years ago, a phenomenon also recorded of Catholic college and university students in general. I hope and pray that this is a misreading of the evidence.

It is appropriate to raise this point in memory of the great Cardinal James Gibbons of Baltimore who, more than a hundred years ago, set the tone for the church in the United States on the subject of social justice. In his famous memorandum to the Holy See in defense of the Knights of Labor—which the late Msgr. John Tracy Ellis characterized as the single most important document in the history of the church in the United States—Cardinal Gibbons wrote:

> And since it is acknowledged by all that the great questions of the future are not those of war, of commerce, or of finance, but the social questions, the questions which concern the improvement of the condition of the great masses of the people, and especially of the working people, it is evidently of supreme importance that the church should always be

found on the side of humanity, of justice toward the multitudes who compose the body of the human family.

Carindal Gibbons was writing at a time when the overwhelming majority of Catholics in the United States were impoverished immigrants. I fear that today when many (but by no means all) American Catholics are more prosperous than their forebears we may fail to realize that poverty is still endemic in our society, especially but not exclusively among minorities. We may also fail to realize that we are still a church of immigrants, perhaps even more so than we were at the end of the nineteenth century. It is estimated that between 1959 and 1989, 3.6 million people, mostly Hispanics, came to the United States legally. Between 1960 and today, millions of immigrants have come from Asia. These numbers do not include refugees and those who came illegally. The late Jesuit Joseph Fitzpatrick of Fordham University, who was a leading Catholic expert on immigration, tells us, "Whenever migrations are in progress, you can be sure that the finger of God is writing, often in strange ways. Our religious history began with a migration, God telling Abraham to leave the land of his father and to go to a strange land where God would make him the father of many nations."

There are those among us those who argue that evangelization of the poor and evangelization of the new immigrants must be exclusively "spiritual." That's a seductive half-truth. The role of the church in addressing the social and economic problems of the new immigrants—and indeed, of all the impoverished people in our affluent society—is admittedly a complex problem, one that leaves ample room for honest differences of opinion about who speaks for the church, under what rubric, or with what degree of specificity, and so on. To state simplistically, however, that the church's evangelization should be exclusively "spiritual" finds no support whatever in the entire corpus of Catholic social teaching, from *Rerum Novarum* of 1891 to Vatican Council II, and, more recently, Pope John Paul II's encyclical *Centesimus Annus*. This encyclical, more emphatically than any of the earlier church documents on Catholic social teaching, clearly and repeatedly states that "The 'new evangelization,' which the modern world urgently needs...must include among its essential elements a proclamation of the church's social doctrine....Thus the church's social teaching is itself a valid instrument for evangelization."

Writing about the role of the church's social teaching in evangelization, Pope John Paul II comes down strongly in favor of a preferential option for the poor, not only in Third World countries but also in the industrialized countries of the West. "In the countries of the West," he says, "different forms of poverty are being experienced by groups which live on the margins of society, by the elderly and the sick, by the victims of consumerism, and even more immediately by so many refugees and migrants." The pope's numerous references to the plight of the unemployed—again, even in the affluent West—are also, needless to add, very timely.

Pope John Paul II was the 1995 Man of the Year in *Time* magazine. In a sidebar article about him, the conservative British Catholic journalist Paul Johnson referred to liberation theology as "quasi heresy." This is not the forum in which to debate the issue of liberation theology with Mr. Johnson, but I think it is appropriate to close on a radically different note. I do so by quoting a passage from a meditation entitled "Concern for the Poor" in a recent book on the psalms by a Spanish Jesuit stationed in India:

> Thank you, Lord, for your gift to your church in our days; the gift of concern for the poor, of awareness of injustice and oppression, of awakening to liberation of the human soul and in the structures of society. Thank you for having shaken us out of our complacency with existing orders, out of acquiescence in equality and temporizing with exploitation. Thank you for the new light and the courage that have surged through your church today to denounce poverty and to right oppression. Thank you for the church of the poor.

I have emphasized the theme of hope throughout this article. I conclude on the same note, in the words of Fr. T. Howland Sanks, a distinguished ecclesiologist teaching at the Jesuit School of Theology in Berkeley. Fr. Sanks recalls that the Christian community has throughout the course of history lived amid a series of polar tensions, between unity and diversity, between the particular churches and the Church Universal, between being a community of the holy and being a school of sinners, and various other tensions. "Knowing this history," he says, "we should not be [threatened] with change today, nor easily let go of our heritage. Our task…is not to survive but to serve, not to worry, but to witness, not to hide but to hope, and to bring hope to others. As Gustavo Gutierrez has said, 'This time is dark only for those who do believe the Lord is present in it.'"

FRANK J. McNULTY

e were lined up in the corridor of the major seminary, nervously waiting for our first interview with the spiritual director. When the first man came out, all those rookies gathered around him. "What did he ask?" One of us vocalized the concern that was in all of us because we were afraid of saying the wrong thing. "He asked me, 'Why do you want to become a priest?'" That was a logical question, but then someone said, "What are you supposed to say?" The smartest guy in the class spoke. When he spoke, you always listened. "I think you're supposed to say, 'to save my soul and the souls of others.'" That sounded good to me. I was near the end of the line, so, by that time, I parroted those words the spiritual director had heard before—several times. He knew the answer had been passed along the line and just smiled.

It was hard to say why I wanted to become a priest. I was attracted to the life, more by what priests do than by their position in the church. What I later learned was ontological. But I knew so little about their life. They helped people and seemed close to God. That's about all I knew. Rectory living, liturgy, daily trials, church politics, activities, training, assignments, role of the bishop—all of that was vague. I didn't even know about the All Souls envelopes or whether you got a salary! I'm reminded of a father I know who tried unsuccessfully to dissuade his son from attending the Naval Academy. Long after the acceptance letter came, the young man asked him, much to the father's chagrin,

"What does a naval officer do?" Now, over fifty years later, knowing a whole lot about priestly life, the question is only somewhat easier because it still involves "stuff" of the heart.

> In a book called *Listening to Your Life,* Frederick Buechner describes a moment from his own life: "I hear you are entering the ministry," the woman said down the long table, meaning no real harm. "Was it your own idea or were you poorly advised?" And the answer that she could not have heard even if I had given it was that it was not an idea at all, neither my own nor anyone else's. It was a lump in the throat. It was an itching in the feet. It was a stirring in the blood at the sound of rain. It was a sickening of the heart at the sight of misery. It was a clamoring of ghosts.

A good chunk of my priesthood was spent teaching in the seminary. In an effort to become more informed, students would sometimes ask me, "What's it really like out there in a parish?" I often found myself saying that I had found the priesthood harder than I thought it would be. But for me, it has been happier than I ever dreamed it might be. Harder and happier.

This is not the occasion to reflect upon the "harder" side of that paradox. As a matter of fact, most lay people I know have found life to be much harder than I have. As an aside, let me say this — If I am to serve *"in persona Christi,"* why should some trial and suffering come as a surprise. On ordination day, the bishop put oil, the symbol of strength, on my hands. And in that oil, he drew a fitting symbol, the cross. So, the journey had some valleys as well as mountaintops.

To begin an answer to why I am still a priest, I would simply say I like what I do! I enjoy it. The extreme workaholic may be too driven, but for most of us the very nature of the task fulfills us and keeps us going. There is a routine and variety, maybe more of the latter than the former. You are anything but a "bean counter" and most of what we do is not dull. I like celebrating Eucharist, especially with a church full of people. I like celebrating other sacraments. I like being there for people, invited into their lives for the big and small moments. An older priest once said to me, "Mac, we ought to be able to cry with them." Yes, and laugh with them, too. I enjoy the challenge of preaching the good news and making it sound good, the challenge of giving them something useful and helpful to bring back into their daily lives.

Sometimes on a priests' retreat, I ask them to share with one another what has kept them in. Many of them simply say, "the people." All I have just written falls under that category, but there is more to it than ministering to them. It has to do with relationships. Ten years ago I was asked to address John Paul II about today's priesthood in our country. One thing I said was this:

> If priests could open up their hearts and tell you of their priesthood, they would speak of God's people. We are eye-witnesses to wonderful things which do not get officially recorded: their enthusiasm, their spirit, their remarkable generosity and especially their genuine love for priests. They understand our humanness, they forgive our failings and they are a constance source of joy. And, with all this, they constantly challenge us to be holy.

Another way of saying it would be the feeling of belonging and what that does for all of us, clergy and lay. Community. The healing power of this community has always impressed me. In that typical Sunday gathering, there are hurts, worries, fears, problems, and crosses, and together we bring it all to that altar. And, often enough, the people bring it to us, their priest, and we listen to their hearts and do what we can. J. F. Powers is a novelist who writes about priests. I asked him once why he was so fascinated. His reply was along these lines: As a priest, you handle the important aspects of life: faith, suffering, life after death, values, sin, virtue. A carpenter handles wood and nails. Think of what passes through your hands. I never quite thought of it that way, but Powers is on target.

We stand with the people in their sorrows and joys. They invite you into their lives and their hearts. You stand with them with no easy answer to the tears, but you are there. As I've gotten older, I have realized the tremendous trust people have placed in me from ordination day on. They have brought me so much, their most intimate thoughts and heart-wrenching problems. Why? Precisely because I am priest. In a failed Broadway show, an older priest expresses his discouragement to a friend. He pauses reflectively and says something I have never forgotten. "But you know...there are some wonderful moments." Just like those few good drives have brought me back to the golf course, those "wonderful moments"—more than a few—have kept me in the priesthood. They are so varied. It is not unusual to celebrate a funeral liturgy in the morning and, on that same spot, a few hours later, a Nuptial Mass. To baptize an infant in the afternoon and that evening to anoint a ninety-year-old. Wonderful moments!

Another plus for me is the priestly fraternity. That sounds a little corny and much like the "old boys club" but that could be the best way to say it. I enjoy priests, find them good company, and, at time, fun to be with. Not all priests fit that description and not all priests enjoy the company of other priests. Some of the present polarity has hurt the fraternity. But being with priests helps me to remain one. Like other groups, there is a subculture with a language and a humor only priests could catch completely. Sit with a group of them during a retreat and listen to the local stories and legends. They get repeated often, change a bit in the telling, but the laughter is genuine.

A word could also be said about creativity. A doctor friend is fascinated with the diagnostic side of medicine and it becomes a challenging adventure for him. I feel that way about priestly ministry. I like searching for better ways of doing things: more effective ways to preach, to organize, to teach, to bring fringe people closer to the center, to make the message attractive, to help family life, to create a good climate in the parish. We can be creative and than can make our ministerial tasks even more rewarding. Not all the ideas work, but it's nice to have the freedom to try them.

If you asked me to sum it all up in one word, I would use the word "ministry." Let me tell you about a movie. It's about a washed-up folk singer. He is a handy man at a motel and falls in love with the owner. Her husband was killed in the war and left her with a young son. The two marry and he tells her one day how happy she has made him. He asks her how it has been for her. She says something like this: "Oh, for me, you and the boy have been God's tender mercies." That's the name of the movie and I can echo her words. For me, the people I minister to and with have been God's tender mercies. Along the way, I hope and pray that this life I have chosen will help me to "save my soul and the souls of others." There is more to it than that, but it's not a bad reason to become a priest.

JOSEPH M. CHAMPLIN

T here are really two questions here: "Why did I decide to become a priest almost a half century ago?" and "Why am I still a priest today after nearly four decades in the ordained ministry?"

No one, including myself, can give a definitive answer to the first inquiry. Our motives are so mixed, every vocation such a mystery, and the human heart so impenetrable that only God knows why an individual takes this step into the seminary and onto the altar.

Pope John Paul II, in his 1992 postsynodal exhortation, describes the profound, complex, and mysterious nature of a priestly call. He says that it, like all vocations, represents the "history of an inexpressible dialogue between God and human beings." It is a "fathomless mystery." It encompasses a "personal and unrepeatable life project."

Having made that disclaimer, I can say that the Eucharist and eucharistic people seemed to be the most significant factors influencing my decision to become a priest.

I grew up in a small New York State village, the product of an interreligious marriage (father Episcopalian, mother Catholic). Despite a divorce, poor health, and financial woes during those depression days, my mother remained close to the church. We always went to Sunday Mass and often on weekdays too. I served at the altar regularly, felt the impact of different good pastors, and was singled out as a potential priest, despite being an active hell-raiser and ardent admirer of girls.

Four maiden aunts were daily communicants and prayed that either my brother or I would become a priest. Since he married and had six children, that sort of sealed my destiny.

When I was twelve, my mother married again (to another Episcopalian) and we moved to his homestead on a Central New York farm. I went to public school in Camden, a dozen miles away. Sometimes in the spring I pedaled my bike that distance so I could practice with our baseball team in the afternoon. On those occasions I usually left home early enough to catch the 8:00 A.M. Mass before classes started.

The pastor at Camden, an avid reader, organist, and lover of the Eucharist, kept alive in various ways that vocational spark within me during turbulent adolescent days. He also forever affected my future by taking me as a young seminarian to Grand Rapids for one of the early Liturgical Weeks. I went annually thereafter for the next 25 years.

The pastor at my tiny home parish in Cleveland, New York, a few miles away from our house, himself a delayed vocation, sometimes would be quite direct with unsolicited advice. While I was a freshman at Yale, for example, I clearly recall Fr. Butler bluntly asking me, "Joe, when are you going to the seminary?" But I also can visualize the care with which he celebrated early morning Masses and his visits at dusk before the Blessed Sacrament. On those latter occasions, he would be kneeling there in overalls and undershirt, bathed in sweat from having mowed the church lawn after supper.

During the final three years of decision making before the seminary—at Andover, Yale, and Notre Dame—frequent daily Mass, often at some inconvenience and, of course, Sunday Eucharist, helped. It enabled an ambivalent young man finally to give a hesitant "yes" to the inner call he first sensed at an early elementary school age.

Since ordination in 1956, I have spent one-third of my priest-hood in administration on the national or diocesan level and two-thirds of it in parish ministry. Just as the Eucharist and eucharistic people were so influential in leading me to the altar, I credit those same factors for the fact that I am still an active priest today.

Extended prayer before the reserved Presence on a regular basis (ideally each day, but for me I'd say 90 percent of the time), has been an essential lifeline. While I have been blessed with enormous successes, accomplishments, and recognition, there has been a balancing amount of weaknesses and wounds, poor choices and burdensome crosses. I don't think I would have sur-vived spiritually without ongoing, extensive prayerful reflection.

The development of a Perpetual Adoration Chapel in our parish with 400 lay people spending an hour each week before the exposed sacrament fits nicely into that pattern. When you enter the chapel for a period of prayer at least one parishioner will always be there. That encourages me: I presume my presence heartens them.

The Liturgical Weeks had an enormous impact upon both my interior and ministerial life. I met, in those early days of wor-ship renewal, people who were real spiritual giants. They loved the liturgy and loved the church. One cannot encounter persons like that without being profoundly touched. Those conference days also gave me an early understanding of the hoped-for liturgi-cal changes, a preparation that would stand in good stead when post–Vatican II reforms began in the late 1960s.

I met the venerable and remarkable late Msgr. Martin Hell-riegel at these weeks, spent a week as a guest at his famous Holy Cross Parish in St. Louis, and never forgot this saintly pioneer's love for the sacred liturgy and the holy sacrifice of the Mass. Blind the last six years of his life and nearly 90, he still presided over the Eucharist and preached every day.

Fr. Fred McManus's invitation to work with him at the NCCB Liturgy Secretariat in 1968, a direct result of a relationship devel-oped at Liturgical Week, set my life on an entirely new course. While at all times continuing to be involved in parish ministry as a resident priest or pastor, I began to teach, lecture, write, and work on worship renewal here and abroad. Those incredibly rich experiences—over a million miles to more than 30,000 clergy—fed my priesthood and I pray helped those who heard or read my words.

But perhaps it is at weekend and weekday Eucharists when we feed the Lord's word and body to spiritually hungry parishioners that I most feel my priesthood sustained and strengthened.

To preach in a way that weds the day's divine message with the people's very human needs; to preside over a carefully prepared and executed eucharistic liturgy; to offer communion, and while doing so, to detect faith in their eyes, to note reverence in their gestures, to invite a personal response, to bless the babes in their arms and the children at their feet; to greet parishioners before and after Mass; to share their joys and stand by them in their sorrows—these are tiring challenges, but deeply satisfying tasks.

The Eucharist seemingly led me to the priesthood decades ago and surely has kept me at the altar now for 38 years. I am grateful to the Lord and to all those eucharistic people who have helped bring this about.

WALTER M. BUNOFSKY, S.V.D.

They had indoor recess that day. As he sat at his desk, his eighth grade teacher, Sr. Cyrilla, beckoned him to her desk. Out of the blue, a question came, one he never dreamed would be directed to him. "Walter, did you ever think of being a priest?"

So began my journey to the priesthood back in 1944. The tiny seed of a possible vocation was planted. At the time my answer to sister's question was negative. I never thought of being a priest. I never "played" priest nor enlisted my younger sister Elaine as my server. In fact, I had the strange, mysterious notion that priests and nuns were born that way.

Although Sr. Cyrilla aroused a bit of curiosity in me with some literature on the priesthood, I went on to public high school in town after my eighth grade graduation. I had no thought of entering any prep seminary.

In April of my freshman year, however, a Divine Word Missionary, Fr. Lawrence Lovasik, came to our parish to give a mission. I attended it. One evening he spoke on the vocation of the priesthood and religious life. To this day I can't recall anything definite about his talk. But from that evening on my desire to be a priest grew stronger each day—in particular, to be a religious priest.

And, so, in September 1946, at age 15, I entered a prep seminary conducted by the Society of the Divine Word. My sense of global mission awareness would grow.

I spent the next 34 years as a missionary in the United States, first as a vocation recruiter for nine years, then as an associate pastor in the African-American apostolate in inner-city parishes in Chicago and St. Louis till 1984.

While at St. Nicholas Parish in St. Louis, I occasionally visited a nearby chapel of perpetual adoration conducted by the Holy Spirit Adoration Sisters (also known as the Pink Sisters because of their beautiful rose-colored habit). At the time, I was troubled. Missing in my life was an inner peace and freedom. I wrote a note and put it into a nearby box. Without identifying myself, I simply wrote: "Please pray for a priest." A few years later, I became their chaplain and remained so for nearly ten years.

From grade school on, I always had a special love and devotion to the presence of Christ in the eucharistic mystery in all its fullness. We used to simply say, "the Blessed Sacrament." But during my years as chaplain of the Pink Sisters, I tried bringing about a balance between the Eucharist *during* and *outside* of Mass. I did this by writing some articles for *Emmanuel* magazine and also some booklets for those who frequent Mount Grace Chapel. I believed there was a reawakening of the need for contemplating the mystery of the Eucharist outside of the celebration of the Mass. And this in the presence of Christ reserved in our tabernacles as our food, healing, and consolation.

My appointment as chaplain proved to be a mixed blessing. In a way I was both running from and toward God. I felt like Jonah, and Mount Grace Chapel was the whale. But whether I was running from or toward God, the good Lord was always in the center with tender loving-mercy. This fact was impressed upon me in my eighth year as chaplain. A series of incidents reminded me very forcibly that God was in charge of my life. I wasn't.

In October 1991 my father died of cancer of the bone marrow. Five months later my mother died of a stroke. A year later a close friend, Eileen, my "first love" in first grade, died suddenly. During this period other forms of death occurred: the tearing down of the prep seminary I entered in 1946, the closing of others where I worked, and the ripping away of a few more significant life-moorings.

But, above all, my own inner turmoil of unresolved personal and emotional problems put me into a severe depression. Down there the light went out. I needed help. No longer would my apparent calm exterior do. No longer could this celibate walk alone or try to figure himself out by himself. "Head" answers no longer worked, whether of past or present vintage. As a bookmark often reminded me: "Just when I had all the answers, they changed the questions on me."

During therapy there were many questions asked and many unattended feelings attended to. Slowly, painfully, I began to climb out of the hole of depression. One of the questions I asked myself and talked about with others was and is the very topic of this article with two words reversed to ask the question: "Why *am* I a priest?" Or to take it back further: "Why did I want to be a priest in the first place?"

I became a priest for a very spiritual reason. I wanted to save my soul. The first question of the catechism made an early and strong impression on me. *God made me to know, love, and serve him, to be happy with him in this life and forever in heaven.* I felt that if I tried to show others the way to God, then I, too, would find the way to heaven.

Being a priest paves no automatic road to heaven. It is my response, made in trust, to God's all-embracing, merciful, and compassionate love for me. With confidence, then, I hope that I am doing "God's work" and not just "working for God." There is a difference!

In the presence of our merciful Lord in the monstrance in Mount Grace Chapel, I often thought how God worked things out in my life. In a way, by becoming the chaplain for a group of cloistered, contemplative nuns, I was running away from myself. And yet, it was there that I found my self. God works things out in *kairos* time and not always in *chronos* time. Or in the words of a spiritual I heard in one of the African-American parishes I served:

"God may not come when *we* want, but he always arrives *on time.*"

One of the monstrances at Mount Grace, about three feet high, is shaped in the form of the cross with a number of rays from the center holding the host. The monstrance reminds me of *kairos* time. The number of rays plus the four points of the cross come to 24, the hours in a day. The sisters have adoration 24 hours a day around the clock. For me, these are not chronological hours but "kairological" (to coin a word).

In Christ's presence we must be open to the *moments* of his grace, given in *his time,* graces for those for whom we pray, particular petitions sought. When and how they are given, we trust in God's beneficent love. In *kairos* time we become more aware that God is in charge of the rhythms of time and life.

Chronos time beats to the rhythm of efficiency—*our* work we set out to do for God. *Kairos* time beats to the rhythm of love— *God's* work as it unfolds and grows in us.

Why I am a priest has much to do with learning more and more each day the rhythms of *kairos* time, God's time, and that all is grace. All is gift. To lay hold of Paul's words, "By the grace of God, I am what I am" (1 Cor 15:10). To be a priest is to be a grace shared with those I serve.

So, whether I "lead" or "show" or "point out" the way to God—our ultimate goal in life—I am as a priest a "priestly conduit, a connecting link between earth and sky." These words jumped out at me while reading *A Woman's Worth* by Marianne Williamson.

She had attended a music concert one night and had experienced as never before "the transcendent way a musician can bring an entire room into a single heartbeat." She goes on to say: "I remember thinking, 'They're priests; that's what they really are. They're priests.'"

Later on she writes:

> After that, I grew more in love with music and live perform-
> ance but, most important, I became enthralled with the idea

that a human being could create a space, through music or anything else, where people's hearts are harmonized and lifted up.

"Where people's hearts are harmonized and lifted up." What a marvelous description of the Eucharist! That moment when gifts of bread and wine, now the body and blood of Christ, are offered and then lifted up to God! What an awesome, wonderful exchange, when Christ is given back to us to form one body, one spirit in him!

What a grace to be part of it as a priest! To participate in such theo-drama in harmonious music and song. May the assembly's great "Amen" resound "like a clap of thunder in a basilica"—to echo Jerome—in *all* our assemblies! In *all* our churches to God's greater honor and glory, now and for all ages...

JAMES E. SHEIL

I really don't know why I am a priest today. At this stage in my life, having served as an army chaplain in Vietnam, spent several years in pain as the result of that tour, and experienced the gift of a serious heart attack, and having been recalled to active duty in the army after 14 years out, I can only stand in awe of the great mystery of God's love for me which he calls me to share.

In many ways I grew up in the priesthood in Vietnam. I recall being on a hill with soldiers waiting for the helicopters to take us to what we expected was a "hot LZ." A young soldier asked to go to confession. He mentioned he was married outside the church, as well as some other complications. I told him there was nothing I could do. At that point he dropped to the ground and cried all over my boots. It was as if Jesus himself was there, asking me who did I think I was deciding whom he would forgive. Needless to say, I heard the soldier's confession. I don't remember anything else about him, but I owe this soldier a tremendous debt of gratitude both for what he taught me and for his kindness to me.

Like most priests, I have had my share of tough times. The awesome experience of giving the homily at my mother's funeral a few years ago was worth all of them. If I have learned anything through my 29 years of being a priest, it has been to let go, to (as the ordination ritual used to say) *"imitamini quod tractatis,"* imitate what we handle, to try to live as an offering to God to be used wherever and however God asks.

To me, the priesthood means the mystery of God wanting to be available to us. The more I can win the battle of letting go, the more I can truly be God's servant. If I see myself as "another Christ," I need to do all I can to be rooted in the Father's love.

I have questioned myself a number of times why I would want to stay a priest. At times I was very close to walking out. Each of these bouts of questioning has led me deeper into the mystery of Jesus' love. While I do not think I have done a very good job of following him, I believe that there is no other option for me. I am profoundly grateful for the gift of the priesthood.

I am currently assigned as Catholic pastor of the American military community of Mannheim/Worms in Germany. With the international situation, worldwide deployments, and the drawdown of the U.S. military, the situation here defies description. There is certainly nothing I have experienced so far that can compare with it.

I am involved in our community in ways relatively unknown in a civilian community. The diminishing number of priests has had a great impact on the military. The requirements stay the same, but the number of priests available to serve gets steadily smaller.

In the midst of all this, I am aware of the power of Eucharist to touch people where they are hurting. Jesus is real. Prayer is an essential ministry. People need to be loved, to be led beyond the pain of day-to-day separation and uncertainty to the reality and experience of God loving them. The only constant is Jesus loving us and bringing us to God.

While I believe a priest is *for others,* I am not always sure what this means. As I get older, I don't think I need to know. I am content to be led often to where I would rather not be, to serve in a way I may not understand.

Celebrating the liturgy and preaching the word have become for me a source of profound joy and satisfaction in ways, in years past, I would not have thought possible. I feel surrounded by the joyous mystery of call and service. I have come to see priesthood as a journey and a relationship rooted in mystery, which goes far beyond anything I may do.

I have noticed a peace in my life that is wonderful. Whether I could experience this peace in another way of life, I don't know. It may be just part of growing older. But I see it as intimately connected with being a priest, with following Jesus wherever he may lead. It has taken more than 29 years of being a priest to get here, and I enjoy it. Whatever the price, the journey has been worth it.

WILTON D. GREGORY

I recently celebrated my twentieth anniversary as a Catholic priest. It was an important moment for me because it represented, at least emotionally if not in fact, the realization of my transition from being a young priest to being a middle-aged priest. It is good for me to write down these reflections, more for my own prayer and meditation than for any spiritual edification for a reader of these perhaps random recollections.

I have never seriously wanted to *be* anything other than a priest for more than 34 years, although my *reasons* for wanting to be a priest have gone through ample alterations, hopefully some respectable refinement, and perhaps even some modest insight over the course of the years.

I entered the Catholic Church as a grammar-school youngster who had become enthralled by this worldwide and yet somehow very personal community of faith. I wanted to be a priest as a youngster because the priests of my home parish were, and thanks be to God still are, such outstanding men. They were respected, wise, compassionate, and obviously quite happy. I knew little about what the priesthood itself demanded beyond the facade of the humanly attractive presence and spiritual mystique of the priests.

As I look back at my teen years, initially being a priest was attractive because of the image I observed in those who pastored my adolescent world. During the 1960s, the church found itself caught up in a moment of renewal and *aggiornamento,* and it was during this time that the images that had sustained my priestly vocation began to be commingled with other reasons for wanting to be a priest. During the same time that I was going through the tumultuous years of my adolescence, the church was experiencing its own transformation. By a strange twist of fate, this church that I love with all my heart was renewing itself with a similar type of adolescent energy, even as I was passing through the threshold of adulthood.

The priesthood then became for me, and perhaps for most of my contemporaries as well, an enthralling adventure of change. Being a priest was being on the cutting edge of tomorrow. Most of the media images of the church and its priesthood were bold and exciting. As a young man, I found the sheer quest of the church in the throes of renewal exhilarating, perhaps because many of those same unsettling transformations were occurring in my person as well. The church captured my heart and my imagination.

One need not dwell too long on the issues that have confronted the church that emerged from the 1960s. The excitement of yesterday has given way to changes that can be observed at every level in the church. There are those who now lament these changes, or some of the results from that renewal. There are more than a few who have lost hope and confidence in the church that has arisen from the Second Vatican Council. Still the church holds a wonderful fascination for me.

Like a great ship that has taken a rather abrupt and significant change in its course, our church has left tempestuous waters in its wake. To be a priest in this church means living with much less certitude than may have marked my life in adolescence. Loving a church that has been ridiculed for all that has changed, condemned for all that still needs to be changed, and criticized for all that is still in the midst of change is no easy task.

I am a priest today for very different reasons than I might even have imagined 34 years ago as a youngster in a Catholic school in the inner city of Chicago. I am a priest for and in a church that continues to be rocked by scandals, impacted by the demands of a multicultural/multilingual society, invited to listen to the concerns of sister believers and to respond to them in the light of the Lord's gospel that both governs our compassion and upholds the church's traditions.

I am a priest today in a church attempting to accommodate the requests of people longing for an experience of a more traditional Catholicism, ministering to a population born in the midst of the sexual revolution of the past generation. I am a priest for a church that is more "suffering" and "militant" than "triumphant!"

I am a priest in a church that has matured from a whirlwind period of renewal. Such a church demands mature love and dedication.

I am a priest today who must love with a seasoned love a people whose profound beauty and goodness must often be discovered rather than being flamboyantly displayed as they once were in the memory of my youth. I am a priest today because I have found in this church a wonderful spiritual richness that can only be appreciated over time.

I have no illusions that our difficulties and challenges will melt away in some magical future moment. My love for our church is not predicated upon a false hope that soon we will return to a state of former grandeur. But in the depth of my heart, I cannot help but believe that the church's best is yet to come—without knowing when or how.

I am a priest today because the church continues to fascinate my soul—even when my heart is saddened and uncertain. At some moment in the future, if that is in God's plan, I will learn to love the church as a senior (that's today's euphemism for the reality of being an *old* priest). How will I grow into that grace? I suspect that it will mean becoming a great deal more forgiving in the sheer confidence that the measure I use to judge others will be the measure used to judge me (Lk 6:38). But that is tomorrow's concern and today has concerns enough of its own (Mt 6:34).

In addition to being a priest today, the church has seen fit to ask me to be a bishop—a call I had far less time to prepare for than the priesthood. But the same reasons for being a priest today seem to me to hold true for the office of bishop. With this added responsibility, I am not only obliged to continue my own journey of conversion but to shepherd, support, and guide others in theirs. And as a bishop, in my service and through my love, I must never allow the church to forget its own wonderful dignity as Christ's own bride!

PHILIP M. CIOPPA

I could never be overly definite as to why I am still a priest eleven years after ordination and four years of formation prior to that. My entry into church life was far from typical and my journey of priesthood has followed the same pattern.

I was raised in a Catholic family, but after receiving the sacrament of confirmation in the sixth grade I decided to no longer be involved in what I perceived to be a very boring church. From that point until my final year of college, I attended church only at Christmas; and even that was not on a regular basis. It was through a very secular event that I was led back to both church and God.

While attending the State University of New York at Albany, I pledged a fraternity. Typical of fraternity life were "keg" parties on Friday nights. At one particular party, after having indulged ourselves in the festivities of that moment, we realized that Lent was rapidly approaching. Since most of us were either fallen-away Catholics or non-practicing Jews, those of us who were Catholic decided to place a bet to see who could survive attending Mass on a consistent basis during Lent. Since I needed money, I was determined!

My return to Mass was an embarrassing, yet upon later reflection, a conversion moment for me. Needless to say, having been distant from church for many years I was unfamiliar with the ritual and content of the liturgy. I stumbled through and even liked what the priest had to say. I decided I could survive another week and returned.

Although this makes very little sense to this day, it was at that time, during the second liturgy I attended, that I made two decisions that would forever change my life. First, I would return to church regularly. Second, I decided there and then that I would be a priest. To this day it makes no sense even as I write. Yet the power of God had to be very present.

Contemplating leaving seminary was a major preoccupation for me during formation years. It was only when St. Bernard's Seminary in Rochester, New York, closed and I was sent to the North American College in Rome that I felt more at peace. By the time diaconate and priesthood ordination dates arrived, I had reached a resolve to be a "loyal" son of the church.

Like New Year's resolutions, religious resolves can also become transformed. After ordination and two years in typical parish life, I became director of the Spanish Apostolate for my diocese. Since that time in 1986, new doors have been opened and my priesthood changed.

My journey has led me to serve as pastor, director of a Catholic Charities agency in my home diocese, director of Catholic Social Services for the Diocese of St. Thomas in the Virgin Islands, and now as regional director for Hispanic Affairs for Episcopal Region XII. What has happened to my spirit of priesthood through all of this?

A better question would be how has my theology and practice of priesthood changed? In the beginning, I was so intent on following every rule and every word of the bishop. I felt everyone should do the same. Yet as my experience changed, so has my vision.

For me, church has never been "easy." I often find myself living church "in spite of…." In spite of the slow movement, in spite of the bishops, in spite of the pope, in spite of other priests, in spite of women religious, and yes…in spite of myself! I struggle on a daily basis more with church than with God, although I have my bad days with God as well. Living without a parish community and working at this level of church has opened my eyes when many times I would like to close them!

Why am I a priest today? I really don't know—it is unclear. However, my faith tells me that God knows. I do have some ideas, however.

I am sure it has a lot to do with Hispanic ministry and the faith I have found among Hispanics. I am sure it has to do with the strength of a woman religious friend who puts up with my ranting and raving. I am sure it has a lot to do with the fact that through it all I pray daily. I am sure it has a lot to do with feeling strongly about making and living a commitment. I am sure it has a lot to do with the fact that I believe the church can change even when it doesn't do so according to my expectations! Most of all, however, I am sure it has to do with the people I have been fortunate to minister to, and with perceiving the movement of God in them.

Why I am a priest today probably is not as powerful a question or statement as what I say to myself each night: with the grace of God, I will be a priest tomorrow.

CHARLES J. RITTY

Why am I a priest? Why am I still a priest to day? "Share the word of God you have received with joy. Meditate on the law of God, believe what you read, teach what you believe, and practice what you teach" (ordination ritual).

"Why are you a priest?" I have been asked that question many times by many different people, including myself. The answer is, "I don't know. I really can't tell." In theology we had a saying: *"Non est mysterium, sed miraculum; non est miraculum sed mysterium."* It is not a mystery but a miracle; it is not a miracle but a mystery. That's about the way it was for my vocation: Mystery? Miracle?

I was ordained in the Diocese of Cleveland in 1943 and celebrated 50 years in the ministry in June 1993. Although I had to retire in 1983 due to multiple sclerosis, it has been a loving, glorious, challenging life, and my illness has not deprived me of the ability to laugh and live fully as a priest.

Certainly the example set by parents and grandparents influences children. In my case, that was doubly true. I was born in western Pennsylvania and was reared in Akron, Ohio, by my parents, Frances Duff and Emil Ritty. I was named for my mother's father, Charles Duff. He was a deacon in the Presbyterian Church; however, he insisted that all his children attend Catholic Sunday School since his wife was Catholic. One day he told my grandmother that he had been to church and received communion.

43

Unknown to her, he had been taking instructions. His action reinforced my conviction that being a priest was my future.

When people asked me as a child what I was going to be when I grew up, I always said I was going to be "a priest of the church." Grandma Ritty also strengthened my desire to become a priest because she had a brother, Fr. Lichtenauer, who was a White Father in Africa. She was very proud of him and was always showing me his picture, an old daguerreotype, in which he was lying in a casket dressed for Mass. I grew up in a home in which there was love and faith.

My mother had a great devotion to St. Ann and named her first child after her. When my father contracted diabetes in 1928, my mother persuaded him to make a pilgrimage to the shrine of St. Anne de Beaupré in Canada. The following year, on July 26, the feast of St. Anne, my mother delivered triplets: two boys and a girl. (My father laughingly said they had made their last trip to St. Anne's!) Sadly, one boy died when only three hours old. They named him Andrew, the closest they could come to Anne. When the babies were six months old, Dad went into a diabetic coma and died at the age of 38. The Depression was in full swing and Mom had her hands full. However, she had great faith and was very resourceful.

The priests and nuns at St. Martha School were also instrumental in pointing me toward the priesthood. Msgr. John A. McKeever was the founding pastor of the parish. He was kind and loving, and encouraged many vocations. Thirty-five priests were ordained from that parish, and many young women entered the convent. At one time it was estimated that ten percent of the graduating students went to the seminary or convent.

One day he told me, "Charles, you will be a priest." This was my first call to the priesthood. He saw to it that tuition was paid to the Catholic high schools and seminary for students whose families were financially strapped, which included me. I also had a football scholarship at St. Vincent High School in Akron, which I attended for three years. In my fourth year he called and said, "You may lose your vocation with all the parties and dances. I think you should go to St. Charles in Baltimore." So I went, although I wasn't too happy about giving up my friends and football.

The three years at St. Charles were the happiest of my life. The friends I made there are still part of my life. The professors, the Sulpician Fathers, influenced my vocation greatly. They were superb, dedicated teachers. After graduation in 1938, I entered St. Mary Seminary in Cleveland. Six years later, 17 men were ordained with me in December 1943.

My first assignment in January 1944 was at a very old Irish parish, St. Patrick's, with Msgr. Duffy. We served three hospitals and five nursing homes, made 900 sick calls in one year, rebuilt an unused hall and turned it into a theater. The activities there helped unite the parishioners in community and strengthened my vocation. It was a joyful beginning.

Then the bishop sent me to The Catholic University in Washington, D.C. to study canon law. I was there for two years and earned my J.C.L., which prepared me for work in the Marriage Tribunal beginning in 1946. This assignment lasted for 16 years, during which time I lived in several different parishes.

The passing years gave me reasons for pride and humility. Each new appointment raised these emotions as I struggled to serve in a new capacity. In 1955 I was named a monsignor. I founded and directed the Diocesan Pastoral Council. As the bishop's delegate to retired priests, I established Issenmann Place, a home for ten retired priests at a period when there were 120 priests over 70 years of age.

My assignments included being vicar for women religious, vicar general of the diocese, and director of diocesan properties. I was chancellor of the diocese from 1963 to 1969 when I asked to be given a parish. Bishop Issenmann sent me to St. Raphael where I stayed for five years. In addition to parish work, I helped to develop the Priest Retirement Fund, and the hospitalization insurance covering priests, nuns, teachers, and lay employees of the diocese, including a retirement plan. One might conclude that I've had just about every job in the diocese with the exception of director of cemeteries. I guess you could say I'm headed toward that now!

I feel that all this work in God's name has brought me closer to God, and perhaps this explains why I am still a priest. I have survived because I enjoyed what I was doing and have been challenged and excited by the many things that have happened to the church and to me. In spite of many health problems, my life has brought much joy to me. Even now, with the aid of a wheelchair, I spend more time with family and friends and like to write for publication.

The Lord has always been with me, drawing me ever closer. More and more, I lean on my Beloved as I await his call and his hand to lift me up, a priest forever, into his kingdom.

RALPH J. FRIEDRICH

Eagerly I read the account of my classmate, Msgr. Charles Ritty, "Why I Am a Priest Today." I did not intend to write my own story. But three weeks later, I visited Charlie dying in the hospital and later attended his funeral. Then I decided I must tell my story, *because of Charlie and others like him.* They are the reasons I am a priest today.

Early years

I begin my story with God and my parents. When I was about to celebrate the twenty-fifth anniversary of my ordination, I overheard my mother tell some of her friends something that I had not heard before. She said that when she was pregnant with me as her first child, she prayed to God that if I were a boy, perhaps I could become a priest. From what I had observed of my father and his constant encouragement of me, he must have joined my mother in that prayer. He died 10 years before my twenty-fifth anniversary. My parents and grandparents, uncles and aunts, my sister, and two brothers always encouraged me before and after ordination by their prayers, words, and deeds.

Even my neighbors not of our own faith had words of respect and encouragement. There was never any advice like some young men may hear today: "Don't become a priest. Don't do it."

Especially helpful were all associates in Catholic grade school and high school, in preparatory seminary and two major seminaries. Priests, sisters, lay teachers, and fellow students were close, supportive friends and examples of Christian living for me, both before and after they heard of my desire to become a priest.

In high school one nun in a private conversation told me her experience as a young woman. She said that when dancing she would sometimes pray, "Lord, don't let me like this fellow too much."

Also in high school I found a special priest—or he found me. Advisor, confessor, and friend to about 20 young men who later became priests, he encouraged me until his death 15 years after my ordination.

After high school I entered the preparatory seminary, and discontinued dating. My vocation then was still not clear to me. I kept asking myself: "Could I become a saint like Thomas More with wife and family, or am I called to celibate priesthood?" My frequent prayer in the chapel, St. Charles, Catonsville, Maryland, was "Lord, guide me in whatever is my vocation, and guide also the young women whom I once dated."

Young Priest

With one classmate, I was the first ordained for the new diocese of Youngstown, Ohio, in 1943. Immediately I felt the friendship of diocesan priests, noted for their spirit of camaraderie. The laity and religious men and women were also supportive. Priestly friendship grew on the occasion of 40 Hours eucharistic celebrations from parish to parish, at least twice a month. Several closer priest friendships also developed at this time.

When Cursillo began in our diocese I realized more the need and help of community, among laity, clergy, and religious men and women. When, our diocese began *priest support groups,* I joined one and continued till I entered Maryknoll as associate priest in

1971, while still remaining a member of my own diocese. I rejoined this support group when I returned from mission and retired at age 75.

Our combined ordination class of 17 priests from Youngstown and Cleveland was very faithful to attending every annual reunion, unless prevented by serious illness or other grave reason. Charlie Ritty was our host last year. We are now nine survivors who will continue to renew our friendship and dedication, and remember those who have gone before us.

Mission

In Central America's El Salvador, Guatemala, and Nicaragua, I found new friends among clergy and laity. Maryknoll Missioners—men and women, lay and religious—held frequent pastoral meetings for ministry and mutual support. The Archdiocese of San Salvador held monthly meetings with a meal for three bishops and seventy-five clergy. Alternate months would be for pastoral topics and spiritual retreat. I cited these examples to Bishop Malone before he approved my second five-year term in mission. He had asked whether I was lonely in mission, and I replied "No," for those reasons. The people we served also encouraged us, especially through small reflection groups and quarterly weekend retreats, called *Encuentros*.

Poor people edified me by their faith and hope amid struggles and persecution. It was my privilege to know and be the friend of many martyrs, including Archbishop Oscar Romero, and Fr. Alfonso Navarro, who was shot and killed in the rectory where I had lived with him ten months earlier. He lived half an hour after being shot. On the way to the hospital he said, "I die for preaching the gospel. I know the authors of my death. Tell them I forgive them."

That was 1977. Three years later, four American women were martyrs in El Salvador, including two Maryknoll nuns and another nun and lay missioner from Cleveland. I knew them all.

Hundreds more gave their lives for the faith, and for serving Christ in the poor. The friendship of persons like these helped me remain a priest to this day.

Meanwhile, my friends in the States continued to support me by encouragement and assurance of their prayer for me and the people I served in mission.

Invisible Friends

The Holy Family was ever present in our family. "Jesus, Mary, and Joseph, make our family like unto yours" was a frequent invocation in times of spiritual or material need, as well as when giving thanks. Mary was close through the family rosary. Joseph the provider and patron of the Christian family was one of us. The Sacred Heart of Jesus was known personally for his unlimited and unconditional love, made especially present through the Eucharist.

Eucharist

My appreciation of the Eucharist began with first communion in grade one. I became an altar server, choir boy, and almost daily communicant during my grade school and high school years.

Ordination was the attainment of one goal, and the beginning of a deeper relationship with God by sharing the priesthood of Christ, with special service to his people. We remember Christ's Last Supper words: "I no longer call you servants, but friends."

Cursillo, which had increased my appreciation of community, also deepened my love of the Eucharist.

In overseas mission among the poor during persecution, the Eucharist became even more relevant. The Vatican II liturgical revisions made Christ more accessible through our native language and through more extensive and varied scripture selections for daily homilies in difficult times.

Summary

Why am I a priest today? Because of *others*. I could not do it alone! Either to begin or continue!

Before I was conceived, God had formed a community of faith in my parents, grandparents, ancestors, and wider faith community. I did not initiate my call. It was God who called me, then hundreds of persons who sustained and encouraged me in early life and 51 years of priesthood.

I am grateful. In the Eucharist I thank God and pray for all who helped. I shall pray and try to encourage others, as God has generously called me. God who called me before I was born, has upheld me directly and through countless other loving persons like Charlie Ritty.

FRANCIS D. COSTA, S.S.S.

A s I look back on my 46 years as a priest, I could never have anticipated all the blessings I have received over those years. I became a world traveler, visiting many regions of this country and many countries overseas, including Africa, India, and the Philippines; I was given the best possible education in preparation for a teaching position in a university; as a member of a worldwide religious community, I enjoyed the close friendship of many dedicated and amiable companions; and, like all priests, I was given almost daily testimony of the appreciation and friendship of many lay people.

I believe my vocation started with the idea that this calling would provide a college education—something my parents could not afford. However, I soon came to admire many priests of the congregation, and their example inspired me to hope to become a priest like them. They were happy and fulfilled, and I felt certain that they did not worry about their salvation!

Of course, my family played a major role in my vocation. Mother and dad were very good Catholics; family prayer was a daily event; my older sister became a religious and she was always enthusiastic about her life. My parents were very proud of her, and although they missed her very much, they were joyful that she was so satisfied and even radiant. I knew that they would feel the same way about me. They told me over and over again that if I wasn't content in the seminary, they would welcome me home with love.

MICHAEL J. HUNT, C.S.P.

For nearly 30 years now, I have served as a Catholic chaplain at secular universities. This ministry has afforded me the challenge and the opportunity to work with some of "the best and the brightest" students and faculty at America's great institutions of higher learning, from Boston University to the University of California at Berkeley to Tufts University. My experience of priesthood has been shaped and formed by the people, the issues, and the problems of the American college campus. In the late 1960s, when I first began to serve as a young priest chaplain, college campuses were convulsed by the issues of civil rights and racism, the war in Viet Nam, and problems of free speech. In more recent years, students' personal problems have come to dominate, from family breakdown to student alcohol and drug abuse to fierce competition for admission to graduate schools of medicine, law, and the other professions. From my perspective of these 30 years on the college campus, everything has changed— and nothing has changed.

A splendid paradox has chased me very personally through these years on four secular college campuses because my early images and my initial attraction to priesthood were formed in a long-ago world that could not be a greater contrast with the places I have served as a priest. In the years between the end of World War II and the election of John Kennedy, I was growing up in an immigrant neighborhood in New York City. The local parish was the center of our religious and social life. Besides attending Mass on Sundays and other feasts, we (and almost everyone we knew) went to the parish school. Athletic teams and leagues organized by the parish provided us with lots to do and much more to talk about. Parish dances and social clubs served all ages from teenagers to senior citizens. These were the years before the Second Vatican Council when Catholic liturgy was stately, formal, and all in Latin and I was one of the hundreds of altar servers who learned a bit of Latin and saw the priest close up.

The priests in my New York parish were Paulist Fathers, revered and often loved by the people of the parish. Young people like myself were drawn to them, basked in their approval, and relished opportunities to spend time with them. I saw in them a way of life that appealed to me greatly and seemed to be as interesting and fascinating as anything a person could want to do with his life. My only reservation was that, as a Paulist, I might be assigned to some place other than New York City, and in those days I could no more imagine being away from New York than I could imagine a squared circle. But even that circle would eventually be squared when I would spend very happy years in California and, before I could count the years, I ended up spending half my priesthood in Boston.

In my early interest and attraction to the Paulists and priesthood, I was vaguely aware that many Paulists served as chaplains on college campuses, but my personal experiences of priests was almost completely formed by the priests of Good Shepherd Parish in the school, in the church hall, working in a parish of immigrants and their children.

Although I couldn't fully appreciate it at the time, my college and seminary education took place at one of those rare moments of grace in human history when the forces of change, culture, and religion converge to create something new in the history of the human spirit. We spent our seminary years at the Paulist seminary in Washington, D.C., during the presidency and assassination of John F. Kennedy, the civil rights era, and, most decisively for us, the years of the Second Vatican Council. The theology we were studying in class was literally on the front page of the morning's newspapers. Even though we were at that time often painfully aware of the strained resources of our educational opportunities, I received an extraordinary education in both secular and religious studies, which I have never once found wanting on my journey through the more exalted spheres of American secular higher education. An immense gratitude wells up within me today as I remember the inspired quality of the education and formation that was provided for me and my contemporaries, along with an amazement at the foresight and dedication of those who nurtured us.

For us then—and I hope still today—it was a matter of vocation. We believed that we were following a call from God to place our lives at God's service in the church as priests. For some of my friends and contemporaries, there were dramatic and intriguing stories of how this vocation had turned lives around and defied all predictable expectations. But not for me. My vocation was present, no less real I believe, but never something that stopped me in my tracks. I was attracted to it. I stayed on in the seminary and became a priest and I have loved it. I see my call from God at work constantly but very quietly manifesting itself in the most ordinary ways. Above all, I recognize the initiative of the call, where it comes from, and why it never once, not even for a moment, was my own doing. There was always, especially when days were difficult or the work seemed boring and tedious, a movement from outside and beyond myself, from someone other than myself, and other than the people I was with. This initiative is a gift I have received but done nothing to merit or accomplish. Its origins are shrouded in the mystery that hovers over the encounter of God and myself, as it hovers over every divine-human contact. But the initiative is unmistakable in its source. It is a highly personal word intimately spoken to me by the living God.

Working mostly with young people in college or graduate school has taught me something about what the priesthood can offer people and, in fact, what the people want from priests. Young people especially look to the church and us for words of meaning, of comfort and hope, sometimes of forgiveness and always the gospel. At times, we need to be part social worker, counselor, or facilitator, but we are always a personal sign, a sacrament, of the God who dwells among his people. In an age of deeply flawed human commitments, we are the enduring sign of God's unfailing commitment. It is an awesome responsibility that requires a deeply rooted inner life for each of us, but it is also the source of our greatest happiness and job satisfaction. If I don't always feel this in myself, I simply look at those priests whose lives and ministry I most admire and I find it there in abundance. And so do the people.

As the priesthood has unfolded in my life, four or five times I have faced a crisis in mind or spirit or, most recently, in my body when I was diagnosed with multiple myeloma cancer in March 1997. At the time, each crisis loomed very large on the horizon of my life and led me to rethink all the assumptions and decisions of a lifetime. I see these crises now not so much as tests, but rather as invitations from God to come closer and to realize what I have always known—that God alone is holy. While each of these crucial episodes in my life is very different from the others, the message is nearly identical: "Be still and know that I am God." Periodically I need to have that said to me and when I am able to hear it, I am healed and renewed. At times, it has taken God quite a bit of effort to get my attention. But each time, eventually, I have responded, and I am priest today because I continue to receive the grace to make that response, and because there is a God.

SYLVESTER D. RYAN

I am a priest because, after my parents and family, I am convinced that my vocation as a priest and bishop is the best gift God could have given me. I say this because as my priestly life has unfolded, I simply love being a priest and I find the ministry of a priest/bishop fulfilling, challenging, and exciting. My life and ministry as a priest/bishop is who I am.

As I have reflected on my experience of a vocation to the priesthood, I realize that the grace of my vocation, like all vocations, developed through significant, though sometimes subtle, aspects and experiences of my life. From the perspective of 41 years as a priest and bishop, I see many elements of my life as integral parts of God's call to be a priest.

In my senior year in high school, our parish of St. Catherine's in the town of Avalon, Santa Catalina Island, California, received a new pastor. He was a man of enormous energy and personality. He brought a lively sense of humor and an entertaining abundance of jokes. People instinctively recognized and responded to his kind wisdom and deep compassion. He called forth people's gifts and encouraged their active involvement in the life of the parish.

He also enjoyed a special gift for preaching, using humor and insight to touch people's hearts. At the same time, he opened up for us marvelous depths and breadth of Catholic thought and culture. He brought with him a splendid library of Catholic and secular books. I found myself fascinated with my first experience of a personal library, one so rich in Catholic literature. I loved spending time in his library reading and browsing, especially when he was looking for me to do some cleanup jobs around the parish.

Most important, his faith and love of Christ and the Eucharist truly nurtured the parish community of St. Catherine's. His reverent, prayerful celebration of the Mass taught me, in an unforgettable way, the central place the Eucharist holds in our Catholic life. In fact, because of his deep devotion to the Eucharist, I began to attend daily Mass. Even to this day, the Eucharist and the word of God remain the primary foundations of my spirituality and ministry.

I had planned, at the end of my senior year in high school, to go to college and study to be a teacher and coach. So after graduation, I set off to a community college "over town," as we islanders spoke of the mainland. I certainly enjoyed my first year of college, its academics, athletics, and social life.

Yet, even while immersed in college life, my pastor's example and inspiration led me to pray and reflect about becoming a priest and whether or not I would be good enough to be one. Finally, by the end of my first year of college, I decided to apply to the archdiocesan seminary to study for the diocesan priesthood.

Nine years later, and unbelievably for me, I was ordained a priest in 1957 for the Archdiocese of Los Angeles. I was assigned to St. Agnes parish in Los Angeles, which included an elementary and high school. I was captivated by parish life, and found myself doing what I originally had thought to be my life work, teaching and coaching. But there was more, much more. The pastor of that first parish was light years ahead regarding the renewal of liturgy, lay leadership formation, the Christian Family Movement, and Young Christian Students. It was an compelling introduction to pastoral ministry!

Not long after my ordination and first assignment began, John XXIII was elected pope and Vatican Council II was convened. My classmates and I maneuvered our way through those early, heady years of the council. Time and many layers of experience have revealed how profoundly these documents and the spirit of the council have molded and continue to shape our Catholic lives and the priestly ministry as well, especially those on the church, liturgy, and revelation.

In my consequent assignments as a teacher, high school principal, college instructor and chaplain I learned even more about administration and collaboration, to add to the zest I felt for parish ministry. I was thrilled, therefore, to be appointed to my first and only pastorate of a parish community.

As their shepherd, I walked with the people of God in our parish in all the daily and critical moments of their lives. My life was crowded with the celebrations of Sunday and feast day liturgies. I loved preaching the word of God week in and week out, celebrating the sacraments, working with teams to implement the RCIA, plan the liturgical seasons, and facilitate the empowerment of the laity in many different ministries. I was graced, as are all pastors, to be present to the people of the parish in the crucial crossroads of their lives, all those joyful, sad, tragic, and triumphant moments that indelibly mark people's paths.

Being ordained a bishop nine years ago and appointed Bishop of Monterey, in central California, has enabled me to shepherd the people of God and lead a diocese in the continuing implementation of the vision of Vatican Council II. It has also called me to a richer personal care about the universal church, both national and international. One unforeseen gift in these later years is that I have been invited to give retreats to priests across the United States. In these retreats I have been impressed and energized by the dedication to the church of so many priests who, at times, face daunting, pastoral tasks.

I am a priest/bishop because of God's grace and call. The hundredfold in my vocation has come in the guise of lasting friendships, multiple pastoral opportunities and challenges, the support and affirmation of friends and family, especially through the tough times, and above all, the privilege to serve our Lord, the church, and the people of God.

JOHN GARTNER, S.S.S.

Why am I a priest today? The answer is rather simple. It's because after all this time, I still feel that the Lord has called and continues to call me to the priesthood much to my constant surprise and against what I would have preferred when I was young. There is nothing that can compare with or replace the feeling that the call continues, and there's joy in its exercise. The call has to be felt as a constant, ongoing process. Unless there is a serious breakdown of enthusiasm (and this can happen), it will always be thus because of God's fidelity.

In the minor seminary, I was always hoping to be told I had no vocation and could go home and get married; but I came from a good family—which is not a bad criterion because it includes more than yourself. My mother, as I look back on it, played a part in my vocation. It was a quiet one, no pressure ever (in fact, I sometimes thought she was indifferent), no gushiness, which usually carries its own message. Now I can see her pride and prayerful attitude always following me when I needed it, even when she did not know the need. She was constant. But Lord stood me on my head and turned all things around when he finally decided to let me hear the call. No regrets in all this time. It was clear and so was my yes.

I'm here and I still have something to do for myself and my priesthood. As long as you can say that, there's always a goal. God certainly had a plan in calling me, and I want to find out if I've understood what it was and if I've gotten there (or even close) and what it has to do with God.

I'm slowly beginning to realize that the priesthood and I are meant to be one and the same, alive and merged together, and that whatever vocation or ministry Jesus calls me to, the main thing is a kind of personal integrity and a striving for the perfect fit between the self and that vocation. I don't think Jesus wants an alter ego to compete with him. The self and the priesthood are not easy to combine into one.

What I still have to accomplish has nothing to do with any ministries I have not engaged in or fields that I've not explored. No priest can be expected to develop everything within his capabilities, or at least within the broad sphere of required priestly activities as they have come down to us from an inflated tradition. We make choices, mostly by temperament.

I do not have the time to lay out an agenda of all I still have not accomplished—sermons not preached or liturgies not celebrated. I have been ordained some 40 years. I'm too old to draw up a program of those areas of involvement and expertise that I've not reached and that I would want for myself on a priestly level. These could include further growth in the liturgy, biblical studies, social justice, special areas of theology, psychology, sociology, economics—new fields, some of them not considered relevant when I first answered the call.

God gave me a good mind, for which I'm grateful, and I could grasp some of the complexities of these fields. I feel that at this time I am beyond "efficient." I'll even say that a priest at any time is beyond "efficient" for efficiency's sake because proficiency tends to build the ego, the self-image, which is more an image than it is the true self. It can be used for the kingdom, but it remains a source of ego-building (to which we must die), unless you become a contemplative and understand your efficiency from a new and supernatural angle of participation in creation and redemption.

When I say that I still have things to do, I'm not aiming at these areas of ministerial development. Rather, I think of the journey I still have to reach within myself, an acceptance or, if needed, a radical change of my own particular priestly perspectives—a sort of interior integration of who I am and what I've actually accomplished, and even of my frailties. Despite the fragility, the call continues, and I have to discern if there is a growth in Christ or a line in the portrait that still remains to be drawn, and what I can do about it. All this leads to a personal identification with the call and with the One who called.

Each call has personal words and we must spend our life in hearing them and knowing what they mean. I still have to sing my "hymn" to the universe and to the One who composed the words and the melody, and I want to find out if I know the melody and the words and if the singing still brings joy.

I'm a Blessed Sacrament priest and the word that used to describe our life was "adorer." Our vocation then was a response to the real presence. Christ was present to us, so we were to be present to him in adoration of the Blessed Sacrament. This is what we learned, and it has a lot to do with the things I still have to accomplish in order to fulfill my yes, my priesthood. I am slowly becoming aware of new ways he is present to me sacramentally, and the question is whether this discovery calls for a new presence of me to him or anyone else. This broadens horizons far beyond the literal meaning of the real presence of Christ in the Eucharist.

Take the notion of presence. Apply it to the life of prayer, worship, and liturgy, and you have to end up with Jesus the Christ present, as our pray-er and worshipper, with whom we are connected in the liturgy. We join and are present to that saving action.

But direct the word "presence" to the community and to all the people to whom he is present and who participate in the Eucharist, and your parameters are greatly enlarged. His presence *per se* isn't, but the scope is. The meaning expands so that interaction with the laity becomes more challenging and opens up new areas where Jesus is sacramentally active and present.

When you discover he is present in his word and speaks to others, you appreciate that you can be identified with his voice and thought. You listen deeply so that you can be a faithful echo. Looking at the assembly, you begin to realize what Jesus' Jewish cultural and religious background must have made him see when he was on earth, and why he made the proclamation in the synagogue at Nazareth, and you ask how you distribute your own presence.

But it's all based on one's attempt to be present to him in the prayer of the liturgy. You draw the consequences of your prayer in the contemplative moment, whether in the liturgy or in prayer.

All this is possible if I weren't a priest or didn't stay one. The expression might be different. I'm not even saying others can't and don't do it better without ordination. But I wonder if the call is not linked to the accomplishment in my life. Fidelity to that original grace remains not only a great thing, it's the only thing. It's between God and me, and I need it to be present to myself, to others, and to the Lord.

JOHN PETER SINGLER

I have often asked myself why I am a priest, and many have asked me the same question. After twelve years of ordination, I remain puzzled, stumped, and yet content with being a priest today, even if I don't completely know why. Why am I a priest today? Why not?

I don't want to sound disrespectful of or even simplistic with regard to priesthood, but as a priest I have found life. Could I have found life in another profession or in another ministry, married and with a family? I can say yes, without a doubt. But why a priest, especially today? Very simply, because I have had the powerful witness of my parents and family and friends to show me a God who takes us as we are and where we are, and I have allowed that witness and grace to lead me to find paths I would not have otherwise followed.

For 30 plus years I have been gifted to recognize through prayer, reflection, and discernment the power and the working of the Spirit of God in my life. That Spirit led me into and out of the seminary high school and college, and then back into the seminary to eventfully graduate and be ordained. This power-filled Spirit led me to open up my eyes, my heart, and my life to seek, to wonder, and, at best, to ask the questions of life and to discover the reality that sometimes questions have no answers. The Spirit has led me through every attempt to live faithfully in the best way possible, and not without a more than fair amount of struggle through personal and family challenges and through various parish assignments. The Spirit has clearly taught me to show and tell others that together we can do the same. Is it any wonder, then, that this Spirit has graced me with the wisdom to begin each celebration of Eucharist and each liturgy with the words, *"How good it is for us to be here!"* (Mk 9:5)?

"How good it is for us to be here," to recognize God working in our lives, and in a different way in and through the word and the sacrament over which I am privileged to preside. How good it is to know God's blessings in our lives and in unique ways to feel and to know God with us—Emmanuel—in the joys and crises of the life I am honored to live. How good it is to rest in the presence of God, especially when running or sitting, when laughing or crying, when embracing or being embraced by another. And truly, how good it is for us to know that whether on *top of the mountain or down in the valley* God is with us. For this we need to celebrate and rejoice! Does priesthood alone offer this awareness, this life, this joy? Of course not. But, for me it has!

True enough, at least for me, no other profession seems to offer the kind of anguish, headache, and heartache, and yet joy, affection, and serenity as does priesthood. In any given day I can dodge the crushing blows of a dissatisfied parishioner as well as witness the miracle of new birth to a family that struggled to create. In any given day I can tremble with the commanding emotions of deep sorrow and profound joy, of anxiety and grief, of death and life. And still in all this I believe, *"How good it is for us to be here!"* Why? Because I know I am not in this alone. With God all things are possible, and this I truly believe.

A bit too simple? Perhaps. A bit too easy? Maybe. A bit like the Lord? I hope so.

True enough, sacramental priesthood is limited and even sometimes short-sighted at this period in our lives with regard to its effects and its vision of God's holy people. There have been too many "It's never been done this way" and "Not in my lifetime" and "You're not listening to me" that would discourage even the most spirited individuals. There are, in truth, too many closed dialogues to even welcome the most open of hearts. But God calls me to covenant, to promise to live in and through and with these discouragements and joys, and to stretch myself out between heaven and earth, as the Lord has done for us.

Has God called me to stretch myself and to offer myself as gift to others? Yes! And God continues to call me to be priest, today and for tomorrow!

ROBERT F. MORNEAU

In the April 9, 1993, issue of *Commonweal,* columnist Kenneth Woodward argues that every student should be forced to ask three interrelated questions: "What's worth doing? What would I like to do? What can I do, given my limitations?"

These questions relate directly to the provocative question of why I am a priest today. If it's possible to answer that question in a single proposition, I would state the following: I'm a priest today because I feel that preaching the word of God, gathering the people for worship, fostering a sense of community, and responding to the call to serve are worth doing.

Preaching is worth doing because words carry truth, the truth about the mystery of God's love and mercy. Proclaiming the gospel and attempting to interpret life's experiences in its light are challenging tasks in our day. Our culture desperately needs another alternative to the values and lifestyles that the dominant culture offers.

Celebrating is worthwhile because when life is not ritualized it remains half-real and loses the weight of its graced gravity. Being present at all the key moments of life—birth, death, marriage, commitment, illness—is a privileged place and time. What is more worthwhile than being at the intersection of grace and human experience.

Gathering people together in community has urgent value in that we need to experience the sharing that breaks our alienation and isolation, that gives us a sense of identity. It is in community, especially faith communities, that love and forgiveness are found. Being part of that community and being partially responsible for its growth is a noble calling.

And service has eternal significance because by carrying one another's burdens and joys we fulfill the law of Christ (Gal 6:2). As priest, I have both the opportunity to serve and to call other people to ministry. Jesus is the model for priesthood, for he is the one who came not to be served, but to serve.

Being a priest today is not without its anguished moments. My heart trembles when I see the gap between what I preach and how I live the gospel. Then there are days (sometimes seasons) when celebrating the sacraments is perfunctory, lacking joy and enthusiasm. Calling people together for prayer and ministry, knowing full well the pockets of division and conflict, causes stress. Inviting others to serve and getting a response from only a few can be discouraging.

Yet the dark side of Christianity in no way diminishes the worthwhileness of priestly ministry. In fact, it is precisely in the "cross"—the apparent failures and frustrations and brokenness—that an opportunity is offered to draw closer to the Lord.

Being a priest *today?* A social analysis embraces positive and negative factors. Technology offers tremendous possibilities of ameliorating the world; technology can also destroy or control our existence. Attempting to bring gospel values to our complex political, economic, social, and cultural circumstances calls for much ingenuity and considerable wisdom. Recent events have lowered the morale of many priests and bishops, so we have to renew our trust in divine Providence.

Some days being a priest doesn't seem to make sense. That experience, however, is part of every vocation and not unique to the priesthood. Doubts, disillusionment, personal failures, a sense of futility are all part of the human condition. No exemptions here. There are "dog days," days one is tempted to abandon it all and travel a road that appears easier.

But God is faithful and, when the call is given, the grace to respond is part of the divine package. The challenge is to remain open to the action of grace and attentive to the opportunities to be an instrument of peace.

South African writer Alan Paton, in his autobiographical work *Toward the Mountain,* records a lesson he received from one of his teachers: "But he taught me one thing, the theme of which will run right through this book, with undertones (or over-tones, I never know which) of victories, defeats, resolutions, betrayals, that life must be used in the service of a cause greater than oneself. This can done by a Christian for two reasons: one is obedience to his Lord, the other is purely pragmatic, namely, that one is going to miss the meaning of life if one doesn't" (New York: Charles Scribner's Sons, 1980, p. 59).

Two reasons why I want to be a priest today: my desire to be obedient to the will of God, knowing full well my many short-comings in this regard, and secondly, my desire not to miss out on the meaning of life.

ANTHONY SCHUELLER, S.S.S.

I have celebrated the eighteenth anniversary of ordination to the priesthood. I find this hard to comprehend. Where have the years gone? And how quickly they've passed! As with Egypt in the days of Joseph, there have been years of plenty and years of challenge. However, I am especially aware of how blessed I am to have been called to serve God and the church as a priest and as a religious.

Looking back on the accumulated years, two events stand out. Both have formed me as a person and as a priest. The first was the death of my mother shortly after my sixth birthday. She suffered from hypertension and diabetes (I can still picture the vials of insulin stored in the refrigerator). Just as vividly I recall the night she died.

Her death left a tremendous void in our family—on two grown sons about to marry, on three minor children, my sisters and I, barely able to understand how profoundly our lives had changed, and on my grieving father. I often wonder what might have happened to our family had mom not died then. Certainly things would have worked out differently, for, as in most families, my mother was the heart and soul, the joy and light of our lives. My sisters, in particular, missed her love and guidance more than any one of us realized or appreciated until years later.

Dealing with death at such an early age made me, I believe, more sensitive to the religious dimension of life and, to the brokenness and pain that are part of being human. My home parish was a small, homogenous community: the extended family of aunts, uncles, cousins, and church helped us get through some difficult times. And the God whose love we found there was a God of compassion.

Many years later (actually it was in my final year of seminary), I had another powerful experience. At that time I was exploring some psychological issues with the help of a counselor. These had surfaced during the previous summer, spent as a chaplain-intern at Children's Memorial Hospital in Buffalo, New York. In the course of these sessions I became aware of my own inner woundedness and how certain unresolved feelings, flowing from a strong sense of sin and unworthiness, hindered my effectiveness as a minister.

As a perfectionist, this was a time of considerable questioning and self-doubt. Through the patience of this counselor, and within the ambience of her care, I came to know for the first time in my life God's *unconditional* love and acceptance, and more importantly, I came to believe in that love as the foundation of my being.

Because of these and similar experiences, I particularly value those moments in ministry when I can express care and compassion. Being a priest is a way to bring God's love and healing to others in an immediate, ultimate sense.

While rummaging through a box of ordination memorabilia recently, I happened upon the following meditation by Teilhard de Chardin, the late Jesuit priest-paleontologist. It expresses my "philosophy" of my priestly ministry:

> To the full extent of my power, because I am a priest, I wish from now on to be the first to become conscious of all that the world loves, pursues, and suffers. I want to be the first to seek, to suffer, and to sympathize; the first to unfold and sacrifice myself; to become more widely human and more nobly of the earth than any of the world's servants.

I am a Blessed Sacrament religious. This, too, shapes the exercise of Christ's priesthood in my life. Number 34 of our *Rule of Life* states, "We seek to understand all human reality in the light of the Eucharist, source and summit of the life of the church." In other words, the Eucharist is the "lens" through which we view life and interpret its meaning.

My most significant and enduring experiences of Jesus Christ have occurred at the eucharistic table, both in celebration and in contemplation. For me, presiding and preaching are not a matter of "performing," but of praying and proclaiming; and times of extended prayer before the Blessed Sacrament—an exigency of our eucharistic vocation—are opportunities for the Spirit to reveal some of the implications of breaking bread with the risen Lord. I see the Eucharist as the most "dangerous memory" of all: it exposes the enormous gap between my professed values and Christian commitment and the way I, in fact, live. Celebrating the Eucharist in truth is risky business!

As an ordained priest, I recognize that I am part of God's priestly people. Ordination demands the affirmation and calling forth of the gifts, talents, and generosity of all the members of the church (in much the same way as the conductor utilizes and orchestrates the artists and sections of a musical ensemble). This is a practical and an ecclesiological necessity today, a reflection both of need and of the very nature of the church as a community of baptized and missioned disciples.

I thank God for having called me to the priesthood and for sustaining me in various ministries and challenges throughout the years. Along with my faith, family, and friends, being a priest is the greatest grace and privilege of my life.

The apostle Paul writes in 2 Corinthians 4:1,6: "Therefore, since we have this ministry through the mercy shown us, we are not discouraged…For God who said, 'Let light shine out of darkness,' has shone in our hearts to bring to light the knowledge of the glory of God on the face of Jesus Christ." To this I add only, "Amen!"

J. G. HANLEY

Why am I a priest today? For the same reason that has impelled me through the past 63 years: a firm conviction that God wants me to serve this way.

I grew up in a small rural community in the Archdiocese of Kingston, Ontario. Our parish never had more than 160 families; yet in the past century it has given the diocese 17 priests, and 35 sisters to various communities.

I attended a Catholic elementary school and got my secondary education as a boarder in a Catholic boy's high school; I obtained a degree in arts from the University of Toronto, through St. Michael's College. During my college course, I had no definite idea of what I would do after graduation. I was sure of only one thing: I was *not* going to a seminary!

However, a combination of developments during my final year made me think that just maybe the Lord might want me to be a priest. I didn't want to do that, but I felt obliged to give it a try for one full year, judging that anything less than that would not be a fair trial. As it turned out, at no point in my four-year theology course could I square it with my conscience to leave.

Although I still didn't *want* to be a priest, I became solidly convinced that such was God's plan for me. During my ordination in 1931, and my first Mass, I felt no emotional thrill whatever. I was simply doing what I believed God wanted me to do. I have been completely happy ever since.

My ministry has included two years on loan to the Archdiocese of Vancouver, teaching in a junior seminary; associate editor and later editor of *The Canadian Register* chain of newspapers for several dioceses for 28 years; chaplain to the Catholic students (Newman Club) at Queen's University for 17 years; a number of diocesan services, including vicar general for 14 years.

At the time I was ordained, no one could have foreseen the Second Vatican Council, which changed our church drastically. But I welcomed every phase of the renewal it inaugurated.

• *Liturgy:* use of the vernacular, and celebrant facing the people; the Eucharistic Prayer read aloud, lay persons participating as lectors and ministers of Communion, the revised funeral rite.

• *Pastoral restructuring:* parish and diocesan councils, enabling laity to have input in decision forming.

• *Ecumenical outreach:* promotion of prayer and dialogue with other Christians and with non-Christians; recognizing what is good in their faith and practice, and sharing ours.

• *Option for the poor:* more responsible use of our resources; we in affluent North America reaching out to help our sisters and brothers in Latin America and Africa.

In these post–Vatican II years, I have not at any time experienced a crisis of identity. I have welcomed the new position of the ordained minister as removed from his pedestal; a vocation of service. I have welcomed the increased participation of the laity; it is no threat to our position.

The obligation of celibacy was accepted in the beginning as part of the package. Before long I realized that it was necessary if one was to fulfill a mission of service; considered as a dedication to God, it gave a luster to ministry. I also realized that if I tried to do all that was expected of me in service to people, I would have been an impossible husband.

In the early years after Vatican II, many priests found it very hard to adjust to the changes in the church, for which their seminary formation had not prepared them. Consequently, a large number resigned from the ministry. Most of those who received their seminary training in the context of the renewed church have been happy in God's service.

As one who has spent roughly half of his priestly life before and half after the council, it has been a great experience. I am thankful to the Lord for turning me around when I was a young man, inviting me aboard, and providing me with an interesting happy life.

FREDERICO J. G. ABLOG, S.S.S.

M y cousin and I were airborne at 30,000 feet, flying home from Toronto to New York City. Spontaneously, I confided to him my intention of becoming a priest. "Boy (his nickname to our relatives), I am going to be a priest." He was astonished! He looked at me askance, his face showing disbelief. Two minutes later, he questioned, "Why?" He was skeptical because I had a stable job working as a vice president and CFO, with a handsome salary. "It's a thank you note to God" was my simple answer.

I thought some more and continued: "God has been good and generous to me, given me the opportunity to travel to Europe and elsewhere, sustained me with good health (I had never been hospitalized), and, worldly speaking, given me a pleasant and enjoyable life. Time now to say thanks to my Great Provider." That was how I felt: the gift of self in flesh and bones. I believed in this authentic articulation of gratitude.

I could have expressed this kind of "thanksgiving" for the gift of life at the age of eleven. I was young and it had never been done. However, it was the beginning of God calling me. Like Samuel, who was awakened from a deep slumber by God's voice, I did not listen nor did I ask God to speak!

I remember when our bishop back in the Philippines came to visit our parish and took the opportunity to recruit vocations for the diocese. He was conversing with my aunt when, all of a sudden, I heard my name mentioned. I ran for home as fast as I could and hid under my mom's bed! That was probably the first call. Not that I did not listen, but I think it was more that I had not been entertaining the thought of being a priest. Or was that the refusal of an invitation?

The second call was when I was in college finishing my bachelor's degree in business administration and accounting. I was then an active member of the University of the East's Student Catholic Action (organization for Catholic students), and very much involved in food and clothing drives for the poor of Tondo in Manila. I also was a catechist in the university-run-elementary school.

These involvements might have prompted our university chaplain, Fr. Eamon Byrne, S.C., to send me to the Vocation Week Program organized by the Missionary Oblates of Mary Immaculate. Consequently, I was among those chosen as potential candidates for priestly studies and seminary life. Fr. Boyle, O.M.I., informed Fr. Byrne of this.

I might have shown some penchant for the priesthood, but, on second thought, declined the Lord's invitation. I knew I was somehow helping preach the gospel by my volunteering to serve the poor and orphans. The bell rang too early! I was not ready. I was afraid.

Several years later I came to America. As a CPA I landed a job first with an auditing firm, then was lured to a higher paying job with Faberge, Inc., as international accountant/auditor. Since I love dancing, I joined the Folklorico Dance Company. I had the chance to perform with the group at Carnegie Hall, Van Wessel Performing Arts Center in Sarasota, Florida, and the United Nations, etc. I was also into disco.

At this stage in my life, I had fallen away from the church. I wasn't going to Sunday Mass or receiving the sacraments. While I thought I had everything I needed, I really wasn't content or fulfilled. There was an emptiness, a void; I felt the allurements of a worldly life could no longer offer me satisfaction, peace, or rest. I was restless inside, starving spiritually. This might have been my daily dying and resurrection. To whom did I turn?

I started attending retreats with the Franciscans almost every month. After a couple of years, I decided to become a priest. I was accepted as a candidate by the Atonement Friars in Graymoor, New York. Again I felt hesitant, afraid. I requested more time to reflect on the decision. I never went back. This was the third call I had declined.

It was along the shore of the tiny islands off Mykonos, Greece, that I came to realize *God loves me.* There was this whispering voice deep within me. All of a sudden I was captivated by the Lord's love; his love seized me. I saw my reflection in the clear greenish-blue water. The little voice seemed to continue, in the words of the familiar passage from John 21:

> Jesus said to Peter, "Simon, son of John, do you love me more than these?" He answered, "Yes, Lord, you know that I love you." He said to him, "Feed my lambs...Tend my sheep...Feed my sheep...When you were younger you dressed yourself and went about where you wanted...Follow me!"

This unveiled everything. God loves me. As a response to that love, in June 1989 I professed perpetual vows in the Congregation of the Blessed Sacrament: "Summoned by the love of God manifested in Jesus Christ...celebrated in the Eucharist, I respond to God's gift with the gift of myself, to live the paschal mystery, to internalize it in prayer before the Blessed Sacrament, and to share with others the life that springs from it." Following Christ was my "thank-you note"—*eucharistein.*

In the Eucharist the good news is proclaimed. It was this spirit of the Eucharist that enabled me to encounter the Lord in the faces of Native Americans in uptown Chicago. I am in solidarity with them in their uprootedness and in their poverty. This was my ministry as a seminarian at the Catholic Theological Union. As I reached out to them, they became my teachers in the ways of compassion and mercy. I saw the face of the suffering Christ in the faces of the many homeless women in the shelter. Jesus' justice, compassion, and mercy were revealed, the opposite of the human law that is oppressive, burdensome, and does not offer hope.

My clinical pastoral education program at Holy Cross Hospital, Salt Lake City, allowed me to be a lifegiver and a caregiver. As a caregiver, it was my task to restore human dignity in time of sickness, and especially with the dying. Being with them in their aloneness and in their loneliness, giving comfort in their trials and suffering. These opportunities enriched my vocation to become truly sensitive to what God is asking of me. For me, to minister is to be *for others* as a Christian. It is grace and salvation.

May 5, 1990, was the day I finally responded to God's persistent call. I have no regrets. I am blessed. I am happy with who I am.

Why am I a priest today? Just recently, I celebrated my fifth anniversary of ordination. The time has sped by quickly, like a passing breeze! Remembering my cousin Eugenio's "Why?" I feel unequivocally that I am an authentic Christian. There is the special joy that comes from serving God and humanity in fulfillment of Jesus' words, "Do this in memory of me." Before, I wanted to be with Christ, but I was afraid to be with him in his suffering and death. I can say that, for now, I commit myself to participate in his paschal mystery, for the sake of the kingdom.

St. Paschal Baylon Parish in suburban Cleveland is my first assignment. Difficulties and trials emerge, the journey is tough. It is a challenge. Truthfully, my duties as an associate pastor have given me a broader theological and spiritual insight and a reflection of the people of God, especially in this parish. My ministries (visiting the sick in hospitals and at home, catechizing pupils in grade school, working with youth, serving as moderator of our singles' organization) allow me to be a true disciple of Christ.

Being a local treasurer (in charge of providing for the needs of my religious community) also becomes a ministry. I have to deal with occasional complaints and even some whining, like the thorn in Paul's side which led him to say, *Christ's grace is enough for me!*

Sacramental celebrations, especially, bring me much closer to God. The life, healing, love, hope, faith, and strength the sacraments bring reveal the real presence of God. Yes, the real presence of God is revealed in the sacraments! In these celebrations I am an active participant in and witness to the manifestations of God. I believe God has chosen me as a conduit of the gospel of hope, faith, and charity. God lives in me and I in God. "It is no longer I who live, but Christ who lives in me."

Why am I a priest today? I wish to "live the mystery of the Eucharist fully, to make known its meaning so that Christ's reign may come, to the glory of God." Thank you, Lord!

JAMES McCULLOUGH

It was late at night. I was 24 years of age, a junior in college, and my mind was in turmoil. I couldn't sleep. I took out a sheet of paper, not to do homework, but to try to organize my thoughts and come to a decision about my future. Drawing a line down the center I separated the sheet into two columns. At the top of the left column I wrote: "Reasons I should become a priest;" at the top of the right column I wrote: "Reasons I should get married," The right column filled rapidly. The left column contained only one entry, yet it was that single entry that proved to be determinative. Allow me to relate what I wrote there and how I came to write it.

Reflecting upon why one became a priest brings back memories of the positive influences of parents, family, and friends. One recalls those marvelous priests and sisters who were such guiding forces in our growing up. In the day-in and day-out growth process, people like that, more than any others, touch our lives, help mold our characters, and help us develop as persons. Our debt to them is unrepayable. But it is outside these that I turn, trying to recapture certain pivotal moments that helped play a role in my final decision about priesthood.

"He's dead," the doctor said on that Friday, April 13, 1928, there at home. "He's dead and she's hemorrhaging, so I'm going to work on her." My body was black. The umbilical cord had wrapped itself around my neck causing oxygen starvation. While the attending nurse and my dad worked on me, the doctor worked on my mother. The nurse and dad got me breathing. Told about this as I grew, I came to believe that such a second chance at life was gift that ought not be wasted.

A hot summer treat of my preadolescent boyhood was to sneak into old Nell Zimmer's backyard to snitch a luscious apple from her tree and a long cool drink from a well, shaded by that tree. Nell often caught me. The penalty I had to pay was that I had to join her and Pete, her brother, on the front porch. There the two of them plied me with questions from the old Baltimore Catechism. I liked Pete and Nell, and I was pretty sharp at that question-answer format of the catechism so I didn't really mind. Of course, bits of candy for correct answers helped too. Today I wonder if God hadn't used them to reinforce my interest and knowledge in the faith?

As I grew toward the tumultuous teens and all that implied, the father of two of my buddies was going to send the two off on a youth retreat, and wanted me to go with them. Money wasn't plentiful in those depression years, so he arranged with my parents that he would pay my way. That was my first experience at making a retreat, and it came at a key time of life. A gesture of generosity, or a more direct movement by God in guiding me?

For eight of my twelve years in parish school I had frequently served at Mass and really enjoyed it. On the first day of my freshman year, the newly appointed assistant pastor called me to the rectory. He handed me a thick folder filled with pages on the new way to serve at Mass and told me to master them. To my astonishment he informed me I was to be head of the altar boys, a position of trust, challenge, and responsibility. God was moving me to ever deeper involvement at the altar.

One Solemn Mass I was standing next to the celebrant immediately after the consecration to be ready to turn the page of the missal, as required. Suddenly I felt overwhelmed with the realization of what was going on. I felt so out of place there, I left and went to kneel on a step. I didn't feel I was ready to be that close to the Lord. That new awareness got me beyond mere task to deeper meanings and stayed with me long after.

After high school and then in the Navy while we were cruising at sea, a number of us would gather in the evening in the Supply Office to exchange ideas and share lives. Often we'd get into discussions on religious issues, and quite frequently I was put into the role of defender of the faith. Some of my buddies even kidded me by calling me "deacon." Looking back now, I see that God wasn't about to let me stray too far during those Navy days and was opening me to sharing the faith with others.

Next came Gannon College, a Catholic College, on the G.I. Bill. It wasn't until my sophomore year that I felt I had academics under sufficient control to branch out in the social and extracurricular life. That was when I met the girl of my dreams. She had everything I'd ever hoped for in a potential wife, and more. Her presence in my life was a gift. She helped me become a better person and helped me believe I had something worthwhile to offer others. Yet, though I did love her, marriage didn't seem quite enough for me; I wanted more. Later I would say: "I wasn't satisfied with being the father of a few; I wanted to be the father of many."

In that same sophomore year I joined the only extracurricular club that interested me, the Catholic Student Action Club. Its membership was about half seminarians and half lay students. Getting to know seminarians and seeing that they were little different than the rest of us helped me see priesthood in a more human and less exalted way. These weren't plaster-of-paris saints but genuine human beings. Maybe there was a chance for me in priesthood. Fr. James Peterson was the chaplain, a man and priest I greatly admired.

In my junior year I was appointed cadet commander of the ROTC. I was elected president of the Catholic Student Action Club. Positions of leadership were being thrust upon me in spite of my hesitations.

One night after a meeting, Fr. Peterson asked me to remain behind. I sensed priesthood was about to be pushed at me again as it had been during high school, and all my defenses rose. He faked me out. Priesthood was never mentioned.

"What are you going to do with your life?" he asked. I muttered something about having two possible careers in mind, the military or teaching. What I didn't tell him then was that in the back of my mind I was thinking that if neither of these satisfied me I might then, and only then, try priesthood. I had confided this to no one; not my family, my girlfriend, nor even my best friends.

He probed again, "And what then?" "Probably get married, have kids and enjoy life," I answered. "And then what?" he continued. "I suppose I'll die; everyone does," I retorted. "Yes," he said rather pointedly, "and then what?" Now I was getting a bit frustrated and more than a bit uncomfortable. I blurted out, "Hopefully I'll get to spend eternity in heaven." "And are you going to take anyone there with you?" he asked.

That question stunned me. Catholics of my era had been taught that the single most important goal of our lives was to save our souls, to get to heaven, with God's help, of course. I had never ever thought of it in terms of taking someone there with me. When I left his office that night, in my heart I knew I was done in. All my resistance to priesthood was dead. I had to come to a decision. I hadn't admitted that to Father that night, but I did admit it to myself.

That was the night I took out that sheet of paper and divided it into two columns and tried to sort out my thoughts. The right column did indeed fill up easily and quickly. That single determinative entry in the left column, the column on priesthood, was an entry I could no longer run away from. I wrote there that night: "Because deep in my heart, when I'm trying to out-argue anyone else, when I'm most honest with myself before God, I have to admit, I truly believe God wants me to become a priest, and I don't know how to say 'no' to God."

Why am I a priest today? I think of the words of Jeremiah: "You duped me, Lord; and I let you dupe me." Truth is, I never had a chance.

Looking back I admire the subtle cleverness God exhibited in allowing me to think that it was I who was doing the deciding, while all the while God was using others to nudge, prod, and guide me toward priesthood. Now, in the twilight of that priesthood I can look back and see the gentle traces of the divine touch bringing me to what God wanted me to be. I'm both humbled and grateful.

I can truthfully say it has been a richly varied and wonderfully fulfilling life, and I wouldn't trade places with anyone. I know that, by the grace of God, I have touched lives. Whether that means I'll be taking anyone to heaven with me is not for me to say or know. That's up to them, and to God. All I know at this stage of my life is that one day yet ahead I must make that final consecration, giving my body, my blood, my life as a final gift for them. God has brought me this far, and God will help me through that as well. Who could ask more of a life?

JOHN MacINNIS

God alone knows why he calls us to our particular vocation. To enable us to discover this call, God leaves clues. We find traces of grace in places where love bears the imprint of both God's name and ours. Looking for such traces in my own life, I see some in the people I will describe as my three families. I notice others in three desires that would not go away.

Three Families

My human family was the first church I knew. It consisted of my father and mother, both now deceased, my brother and two sisters, and a small extended family. In my childhood, we were church in quiet, ordinary ways: Sunday Mass every week, bedtime prayers, blessings at meals on special occasions, a rosary together in the month of May. Through these familiar patterns of devotional faith came an abiding sense of God's presence.

God was somehow *always* there. God was there in the sunlight: in games and achievements at school, in camping adventures, in family vacations at the seashore. God was there, too, in the shadows: in my grandmother's agonizing illness, in my father's sudden death, in my brother's perplexing disability.

Through such days and nights, I learned how to believe and to trust, how to care and to be cared for. God's plan would show itself in other circles of people. But the members of my family were the ones who first opened the doors of simple faith and faithful love. They are the ones who keep them open, years later.

The church became a second family when parish, parochial schools, and seminary drew me out and increasingly further from home. Each of these gave me glimpses of the church as family. I recall breaking the news that I would enter the seminary. A high school classmate, then contemplating marriage, told me, "The church will be your spouse, John, and your family." At the time I shrugged it off as just a pious metaphor.

To my amazement, his prediction came true in the parishes, the campus, and the seminaries that have been home to me. In these places the struggling seminarian, the persevering young woman, and the failing elderly parent, each striving to do God's will, became for me the "brother and sister and mother" Jesus himself claimed as his true kin (Mt 12:50). Add to these the gifted women and men with whom I have worked in ministry. More than just the work we share, it is a wholehearted love for the Lord and the church that relates us so closely.

The family of priests is unique: all men! Several "fathers" came first, then a multitude of brothers. Even in memory, the spiritual fathers of my youth loom larger than life—the gentle, reserved, older pastor whom I regarded with awe and occasional trepidation; the dynamic younger "curate" who took me to the college seminary one day (I knew immediately I had to go there!); seminary teachers and spiritual guides over the years—each spoke of and modeled Jesus: the Christ, the God-man, the Lord and Friend, who would ask of me what he asked of them: "nothing less than everything."

With ordination, this family of priests became brothers I have known and loved for a few or many years. We share a rare gift of fraternity. Because we belong to the Lord, we belong to one another. How could I have really understood priestly life, or survived the inevitable bouts of loneliness and temptation, or experienced the joy of celibate intimacy in the Lord, were it not for these men, my friends and colleagues?

Three Desires

A wise spiritual director periodically inquired of me, "John, what is it you *really* desire?" Guiding me along the path of discernment, he knew that I had to go deeper than my passing wants. I discovered three persistent tugs. At first they pulled me toward something I thought I wanted to do more than anything else. Eventually, they led me to the Someone that I was really looking for: Christ, the one true Priest.

There was a desire to speak of God, to stand before others with a word from God that might make a difference. Like many of my contemporaries, I chose for one of my ordination cards these words of Karl Rahner describing the ministry of the priest:

> Must not some one of us say something
> about God, about Eternal Life,
> about the majesty of Grace in our sanctified being;
> Must not some one of us speak of sin,
> the judgment and mercy of God?

Preaching remains a humbling and compelling force. Every homily presses me inward and outward, to encounter that saving Lord I must proclaim to others.

Another desire was to celebrate the mysteries of faith. I felt this as an altar boy, intrigued by the sanctuary and its sacred contents, captivated by the mysterious language of liturgy, the solemn rituals that marked life and death, love and sin. Over 28 years of priesthood, the yearning and the sense of undeserved honor to gather with the Lord's people, to preside at his table, to wash and anoint and reconcile and unite in his name, to stand humbly before the mystery of his presence, has grown only deeper and more intense.

Finally, there was a desire to lead and guide the people of God. In earlier years, I longed for the day when I could run the show and call the shots as a man with "authority from God."

Slowly, at times reluctantly, I realized that a priest is to lead "as one who serves."

Sacrificing my wishes to the Lord's will for the good of his people, I am still learning to let the Spirit be the leader and guide. Priestly leadership now means partnership; it means harvesting skills and motivating people to work together not for my sake or theirs, but for the sake of the kingdom of God.

So, why am I a priest? I am a priest today because, with inscrutable wisdom and mercy, God surrounded me with these people and planted in me these desires to serve. It was not through any audible voice that he called, but through love. Through the love that people brought to me, and through love for serving them in priestly ministry, the Lord has brought me to himself, and to the true self which is the gift of his call.

EUGENE LAVERDIERE, S.S.S.

hy am I a priest? The answer is quite simple! Like a mystery is simple, like being alive and having friends.

Life is a blessing. So are friendship and creativity. The priesthood, like baptism, is a grace. Blessings enable us to fulfill our potential as human beings. Grace gives us a new potential.

I did not choose baptism. I was called to it from my mother's womb. But today, 58 years later, I accept baptism. Baptism makes me a child of God, a brother to millions of brothers and sisters in Christ, people of every race and nation, all in the family of God.

Nor did I choose priesthood. I was called to it, and I said "yes," as the first disciples said "yes" to Christ and followed him. At my ordination, I became a presbyter, in Greek *presbuteros,* an elder. I became an older brother! That was in 1964. I was 28, very young to be an older brother to people twice and three times my age.

I also became a priest, in Latin sacerdos, a person who represents Christ leading the church. The most important thing I do as a priest is celebrate the Eucharist in the midst of the assembly.

Grace, according to ancient wisdom, builds on blessing. God prepares the work of grace, like an artist prepares the canvas, a sculptor dresses the stone, and a potter kneads the clay.

So why am I a priest? What prepared me to say "yes," not just at the time of my ordination, but more than 30 years later.

I do not know why I first accepted to be a priest. I could not imagine anything else. I was happy. It seemed right.

I come from a great, ordinary family. I am quite certain of this, that the disposition to say "yes" to God came from my mother and father who, in my eyes, as son, have always said "yes" to God, as a married couple, as parents of four children, and as grandparents of three.

I suspect my sister, Claudette, a woman of Maryknoll, my brother Gary, a brother in the Congregation of the Blessed Sacrament, would say the same about their "yes" to God. So would my younger brother Peter regarding his marriage to Cheryl and their children.

It is really something to be able to affirm that your parents keep saying "yes" to God after 60 years of married life.

Friends have often told me, in case I wondered, that my commitment to celibacy is very important to them in their marriage. It gives them strength to be faithful to one another and as parents.

Vice versa, their fidelity as a couple—beginning with my parents—is a great source of strength to me as a priest.

Others, too, help me say "yes" to the grace of priesthood and the new potential it brings, allowing Christ to speak the gospel through me and give life to others. As an older brother to countless siblings, the majority of whom I shall meet only in heaven, I have a personal responsibility to represent Christ among them as a leader in the church.

Yes, I do sense my limitations in fulfilling those responsibilities, but "by the grace of God I am what I am, and his grace to me has not been ineffective" (1 Cor 15:10).

I also feel called to a special priestly mission in the church, to help people understand and live the word of God, to show its relationship to the Eucharist, to minister to brother priests, to open the eyes of all to our missionary challenge as a people of gospel and sacrament, to nurture lay people to minister to the community as did Simon Peter's mother-in-law. How else shall we be good, credible witnesses in Christ's mission of grace and peace?

In all of this, one person stands out above all, quietly but persistently leading me to say "yes" to God. Uncle Willy, a truly great priest, was for me an earthly counterpart of Francis Thompson's "Hound of Heaven," chasing me "down the nights and down the days."

Uncle Willy died in 1991. Fr. Francis Costa, S.S.S., helped me give the homily at his funeral. Uncle Willy had written to me shortly before he died. I did not feel able to read that letter in my homily. Fr. Costa did it for me. Thank you, Frank! Uncle Willy is still chasing me "down the arches of the years." So is Fr. Francis Costa.

Life is a blessing. Baptism is a grace. So is the priesthood. As a grace, the priesthood, like baptism, is also a debt, one of those that never can be repaid, a debt of gratitude, keeping after me to say "yes" every day in thanksgiving—Eucharist—and prayer.

As I said to those who gathered 30 years ago for my ordination and first Mass, I say to all those whose "yes" prompts me today over and over to say "yes" to the priesthood, "I give thanks to my God at every remembrance of you, praying always with joy in my every prayer for all of you, because of your partnership for the gospel from the first day until now…It is right that I should think this way about all of you, because I hold you in my heart, you who are partners with me in grace" (Phil 1:34–35, 7). Amen and amen!

THOMAS J. MORGAN

I am often asked, "Father, how did you ever become a priest and how did you end up in Pennsville, New Jersey?"

In any attempt to answer this question, I realize it is not easy to reimagine and reconstruct the past. It is not easy to immerse oneself in the past because there is always the danger that something has been repressed. It is not easy to go into the dark cave of the subconscious and recover the past.

There is always a danger when we look back to read into the past something that was not there. There is always the danger to see in the past something that is not true. There is always the danger that we will not be able to include the denied, painful part of ourselves, and hence offer an incomplete picture of the past.

Yet, I think it is true to say that my childhood experiences and adolescent experiences in Ireland, with the grace of God, had a great impact on my decision to become a priest.

Even though a vocation is basically a call from God, it emerges in its human dimensions from a whole complex of influences including childhood and adolescent experiences in the context of family life, parish life, and diocesan life, "God always calls his priests from specific human and ecclesial contexts which inevitably influence them" (*Pastores Dabo Vobis,* John Paul II, 1992).

I grew up on a mixed farm. I grew up on a farm where sheep, pigs, horses and cows were raised. I grew up very close to nature and very close to God. The milking of cows each morning before going to school and the feeding of sheep each afternoon was done with the regularity of a paper boy on his route.

The frequent trips on the tractor with my father as he drove through the farm or as he drove to the market were always prefaced with a sign of the cross and three Hail Marys. These were strong reminders that God is always with us, that it is in God that we live and move and have our being. These moments of grace were ongoing reminders that God never coerces us, but always respects our freedom and choices, "The gift of God does not cancel human freedom; instead it gives rise to freedom; it develops freedom and demands freedom" (ibid.).

My mother's commitment to the first Friday devotions and to the First Saturday devotions in hail, rain or snow were a concrete, visible sign of her commitment, reverence, and fidelity to the great gift of the Eucharist. Her tender and consistent devotion to the nightly family rosary and our annual visits to Our Lady's Shrine of Monk always left me with a sense of wonder about life and what was beyond this life.

The beautiful and attractively framed picture of a priest celebrating the Eucharist that hung on our kitchen wall was eye-catching for me. It vividly portrayed a priest raising the host at the consecration of the Mass, with angels descending from heaven and two altar boys kneeling on either side of the priest, reverently holding the end of his chasuble.

I was always attracted to that picture. That scene encased in a large gold frame often haunted me and hunted me. As a little boy, I often fantasized about becoming an altar server some day. As a visual learner, it left a powerful imprint on my imagination. That picture, more than anything else I can remember, placed the idea of priesthood in my mind. It caused me to think a lot about my future. I felt drawn to the Eucharist and drawn to the priesthood, although I was never really certain that this is what I wanted to do with my life.

We never missed Sunday worship. My parents always made sure that the whole family went to Mass every Sunday. It was unheard of not to attend Mass and the monthly holy hour in our parish church. "We have a grave responsibility to cooperate in the action of God, who calls, and to contribute toward creating and preserving the conditions in which the good seed sown by God can take root and bring forth abundant fruit" (ibid.).

My next door neighbors never missed Sunday worship either. They would frequently ride their bicycles to daily Mass and always did the First Fridays and First Saturdays of the month. They were exceptional people, very holy people. The three of them lived in a small, thatched cabin—widowed mother in her 70s and her son and daughter in their 40s. They lived simply on very little. They were loving, nurturing, and supportive of me.

These people loved the sacred scriptures. They had an old, well-used Bible from which they would read about the life of Jesus Christ and would talk about the stories and parables Jesus taught. They would talk about his forgiveness, compassion, and love. I always felt special and unique in their presence. They knew how to rejoice when I rejoiced and how to be sad when I was sad. They knew how to inspire me and challenge me to be the best I could be. They were not only close geographically, but also emotionally, to all of my family.

I think that my childhood and adolescent experiences challenged me to live out my human calling in life, which is a calling to grow, to develop, to mature. These same childhood and adolescent experiences challenged me to live out my baptismal calling, to live a holy, simple, and pure life.

These childhood and adolescent experiences influenced the way I choose to live out my specific calling in life. A priest is called to promote unity and reconciliation within himself, with others, and with God.

In effect, I am a priest today because of God's graced invitation to consecrate my energies to a life of feeding people with the bread of life and the word of life. I am a priest because of the values I internalized and the needs that were environmentally present in my childhood and adolescent years.

Looking back, I realize that goodness and Christian values were all around me. The goodness and values came through my family, neighbors, and many other sources that were hard to see and very hard to accept at the time. These experiences gradually drew me to the conviction that there was a loving God, and that this life was short and that eternity was forever. These childhood and adolescent happenings drew me to the God who abides in all of us and caused me to long for a meaning that no human person could ever provide.

Ordination came at the end of much searching and examining. It was also the beginning of a new way of life and the departure from my homeland. For me, it was setting sail into the open sea without knowing where there could be deep or shallow waters; stormy or calm waters. I knew God had been there in the past. This led me to trust that God would be there in the future. God's love and strength had always been greater than my own love and strength. It led me to rely on God's fidelity and my people's prayers as I tried to see God in all things; as I tried to continue to develop fully my own ministerial talents. It led me to empower others to think for themselves and have a readiness to place their talents at the service of their brothers and sisters for the greater glory of God.

I pray that I will always have the grace to be faithful to the gift God has given me and to respond to the call for daily conversion which comes with the gift itself.

RICHARD BELL, M.M.

As I write this, it is December 3, the feast of St. Francis Xavier. I am writing from Taiwan, from Hou Li Catholic Mission where I have served for many years.

I am a missionary priest. I am also Chinese, and my mission is to the people of Taiwan.

Why did I become a priest?

Experiencing God's holiness and Christian joy in the missionaries I met while I was still a boy had a great influence on me. So did the terrible poverty and the evil I saw all around me.

For me, the priesthood means being close to God, enjoying and sharing God's love and peace.

Here is how I got to priesthood. Someone else did the planning.

From the time I was a lad, I always wanted to be just like my father, who was a wealthy American businessman in Shanghai, China. That is where I was born, in 1927, one of 16 children.

My parents also were born in Shanghai, in the waning years of the Ch'ing Dynasty. At the time, Shanghai was a great international city, the world's gateway to China and China's gateway to the world. After their marriage in 1910, they spent their honeymoon on a trip around the world. They returned to Shanghai to raise a Catholic family.

When my parents married, China was still ruled from the Forbidden City at the heart of Peking (today's Beijing).

Ours was—and still is—a conservative, orthodox Catholic family.

When my mother was carrying her twelfth child, a specialist, a German doctor, told her, "Mrs. Bell, you cannot have any more children or you may die, and the one you are now carrying may die after birth." Sam died a few hours after birth, but less than a year later I came along. Needless to say, my mother had a very difficult pregnancy, and I was born sickly and scrawny. But you should see me now!

Being quite weak, I was my father's special favorite. As far back as I can remember, I always followed my father around, and he took me wherever he could. It was a unique relationship, and my 15 brothers and sisters knew it.

We lived in a palatial estate with racing stables, a swimming pool, tennis courts, and 36 servants.

My mother, who was a convert from Presbyterianism, was a daily communicant and made sure our home was open to all the missionaries that either served or were visiting Shanghai. I cannot remember a meal at home with just the family. There were always guests, and our three cooks usually set a fine table. The Number 3 Cook prepared the food for my father's prized hunting dogs!

From my kindergarten year, my father was grooming me to be like himself. At the age of five, I had a personal bank account with him and was drawing monthly interest. He told me how he made his fortune and how to make smart investments. "When you invest, be sure the company is an old, reputable firm, not some fly-by-night." That stayed with me. Eventually I invested my life in the Catholic priesthood!

When old enough to keep up, I accompanied my father on hunting trips. Just being with him was like the joy of heaven. When I shot my first pheasant, he said, "Good boy, good boy!" And for me this was like God stroking my head.

My father was a great figure in my life. But far more important in relation to God's calling me was the influence of my saintly mother. We often prayed the rosary and for special occasions we had the family rosary in the evenings.

As was my mother's custom, when each of us turned six, she helped prepare us for first communion and confirmation. After she received communion, she would take me, as she did the others, and together we would pray to Jesus in the Eucharist. This preparation awakened in me a personal relationship with Jesus Christ. Communion and the Mass were transforming events. Prayer to our Lord, to Mary his mother, and the saints came naturally.

My mother came from Protestant missionary stock. Her mother was trained and educated at Western Female Seminary in Boston shortly after the American Civil War. I think that is how our home became a home for all missionaries. Many of those dedicated people who stayed or visited with us left their mark on me. I remember them well.

There was an Italian priest who acted strangely at the dinner table. He was on his way back to Italy after being captured and tortured by the communists in the interior of China.

There was Fr. Van Dyke, a Belgian Scheut priest who had been in the interior of China for 40 years. His later years were in Outer Mongolia, until his superior called him to Shanghai. It took him one year to arrive. He walked all the way.

In 1938 he came to our home and lived with us for several months as he had no other place to stay. He accompanied us to our summer home in Tsing Taoy in northern China.

One day we kids were going by bicycle into town to see a movie. We were all excited and ready to leave, and Fr. Van Dyke asked us where we were going. We said we were going to see a movie. "What is a movie?" he asked. Here was this lovable man in his late sixties and he had never seen a movie! So we went in a horse-drawn carriage to see Grace Moore and Cary Grant in "One Night of Love." He was so thrilled at this musical that some of us had to take him again the next day, and several times again!

Then came Pearl Harbor, and all the Americans in Shanghai became *de facto* enemies of the imperial Japanese. We were interned in a concentration camp, which was surrounded by a moat and barbed wire and patrolled by guards and police dogs. We had lost everything except what we could carry on our backs, but my mother thought we were in "seventh heaven" because there were about 100 nuns and priests who had already been locked up before us. All were from the interior of China.

In December 1943, my mother and the younger half of our family arrived in New York aboard the *MS Gripsholm.*

Shortly after we got to the United States, I received a scholarship from the Henry Ford Trade and Engineering School in Dearborn, Michigan. That is when my life took a dramatic turn. I suddenly decided to join Maryknoll, the American Foreign Mission Society, whose main focus at the time was the mission in China. With my Chinese and Catholic background, and with my early exposure to missionaries, it was very clear. That is what I had to do.

I joined Maryknoll in 1947, and in 1957 was ordained at Maryknoll, New York. On the day of ordination, one of my guests was a retired Maryknoll priest, Fr. Ed Mueth. I had never met him, but my mother insisted he be one of the guests. That day, after my ordination, I learned from both of them that, 30 years before, when I was a sickly, scrawny infant, Fr. Mueth had visited our home and consecrated me to Our Lady of Maryknoll.

As you can see, I never planned to be a priest, but someone else was pulling the strings!

Since ordination, I have served in Taiwan, China, where I am now pastor of Our Lady Queen of the Universe Church in Hou Li.

I never planned to be a priest. For much of my life, it never occurred to me to be a priest, but I am mighty happy that I was pulled in that direction.

What better way to be fully alive than to let God pull the strings and follow wherever God wills. What better way to be fully alive than to share the gift of faith I have received?

The gift of faith came to me in China, and that is where I share it, offering Mass, blessing, serving, announcing the gospel, and teaching with the assurance of Christ's abiding presence.

My life has been an amazing journey, from a palatial home in Shanghai to a mission house in Hou Li! I never could have planned it.

WALTER A. RIENDEAU, S.S.S.

" Stir into flame the gift of God that you have through the imposition of my hands" (2 Tm 1:6). A flame begins with a spark. From my earliest boyhood, I experienced the spark of a vocation to the priesthood. When questioned "what I wanted to be when I grew up," my answer was always—a priest!

I do not recall anyone having ever spoken to me about a vocation to the priesthood—neither my parents, nor the nuns in school, nor the priests in my parish. Perhaps they took it for granted that my mind was made up, or that I would grow out of that desire. Nonetheless, I feel that my devout Catholic parents, the wonderful nuns in school, and the priests in my parish did influence my vocation by the example of their lives. I wanted to be like all of them, a fervent Catholic. And I especially wanted to be like the priests in my parish, who evidently loved the priesthood.

Through the seminary years, the idea that a priestly vocation was a call from God and from the church surfaced. I did not particularly feel at that time that I was "called" by God. *I* wanted to be a priest, and I did not sense that God was calling me. After all, God did call the prophets and give them a mission. I did not consider myself to be in the same league as those holy people.

After years of study and preparation, I was finally ordained on September 23, 1950, in my own parish church, St. Aloysius, in Cleveland, Ohio. The spark became a flame. I was now a priest, ready to convert the whole world. Looking back over the past 44 years, I am amused by that idealistic and moralistic young man!

Today, I am convinced that a vocation to the priesthood is indeed a call from God. I am convinced that the call also includes a mission like that of the prophets of old. The mission was the various ministries that God in divine Providence called upon me to exercise: seminary professor, formation director, major superior, hospital and prison chaplain, pastor of four different parishes in three states. Each of these ministries taught me what it means to be a priest, a man for others. Slowly I came to realize that the flame I had been stirring up was my own ego—*I* wanted to be a priest—when it should have been the "gift of God," God, the Holy Spirit.

Allowing the Spirit to guide me in my ministry, I was awakened and awed by the wonders of God's grace. Through me, God strengthened the strong, encouraged the weak, consoled the sorrowing, relieved the troubled, and freed the enslaved.

Conscious of my own personal imperfections and sins, the "through me" never was a source of pride. I recalled how God used Balaam's ass for the good of the people of Israel. Luke's parable of the useless servant, who did no more than his duty, also motivated me. The spirituality of my order's founder, Peter Julian Eymard, encouraged me to emulate his *Absque sui proprio,* the gift of oneself. And since I share in the priesthood of Jesus, the great high priest, like him I must come to my ministries to serve, not to be served.

Another grace that sustains my vocation is the fraternity of priests. I have been inspired by my brother priests in the Blessed Sacrament Congregation, as well as by members of the diocesan clergy and other religious orders. The fraternity of priests leads me to pray for priests experiencing an identity crisis. My prayers also include those priests who are no longer allowed an active ministry because of laicization or some serious moral transgression.

How can I thank the good Lord for my dual vocation as priest and religious, which centers my whole life and ministry on the holy Eucharist? The year 2000 is rapidly approaching, and with it the golden anniversary of my ordination. Now that I have lived the biblical three-score-and-ten, I hope the Lord will give the added years to celebrate my anniversary.

As long as I have reasonably good health, and my superiors permit, I intend to remain in the active ministry. When Billy Graham was asked about his retirement, he replied that nowhere in scripture is there any account that the apostles retired. The example of Pope John Paul II, who in his mid-seventies travels worldwide to bring the good news to the nations, impresses me deeply

Why am I a priest today? Because God willed it! Thanks be to God for the spark that became a flame; and the flame is the Holy Spirit, the gift of God, who guides my life and ministry.

DONALD B. COZZENS

It was a painful day, the kind that lingers in the corridors of memory. This afternoon I told a senior priest that he had been accused of sexual misconduct with a minor and with these words I brought his world to a sudden halt. There was fear in his eyes that reflected the knot in his stomach. Our conversation was awkward and guarded. We both understood that this was the beginning of an ordeal.

The hour in his rectory was particularly painful. The specifics of the complaint were still unfolding; they would surface in the weeks that followed. As I sat there I thought: in front of me sits a man whose lifetime as a priest hangs in the balance. I remember a chilling silence as he read a brief description of the allegation. The twelve years I previously had spent as a professor of psychology told me what to look for in the eyes of accused priests. But there was too much pain to do anything but sit quietly in his presence and gently remind him of his lifetime of service and fidelity. And what was going on in the soul of the man making the allegation? There was this unspeakable sadness.

During the pauses in our conversation, I found myself praying for this good man in front of me, and for the person making the allegation. The prayer gives way to confusion and I ask God to help me understand what was happening in the priesthood during this last decade of the twentieth century. As Vicar for Clergy and Religious, I see up close the pain and the privilege of priesthood and ministry, for ministry relentlessly reveals the joys and sorrows of the human condition and the brokenness and grandeur of the human spirit. You might say my present assignment is to be priest to my brother priests, to be minister to ministers. It is a humbling task that has led to a deeper sense of the healing and reconciling powers of Jesus' Spirit and of the priesthood. I know I pray differently for my brother priests; I believe I pray with greater charity and compassion. Their lives are far, far more difficult than I suspected.

Why do I remain a priest? I regularly ask priests who have chosen to step away from ministry to help me understand why they are leaving. (Priests resigning from active ministry or taking leaves of absence meet with me as a matter of course in the transition process.) Some are willing to tell me their stories.

The reasons for leaving active ministry really aren't many, but they are complex. Most often they are personal: the overwhelming discovery that they are in love, the persistent feeling that they are called to marriage and fatherhood, the almost unbearable sting of loneliness, the acknowledgement that the priesthood no longer makes sense to them, the bone weariness of worry and work that saps reserves of energy and leaves the priest feeling spent and confused.

Sometimes the reasons are theological in nature—the church's position on issues relating to women or ecclesiologies that challenge their sense of priestly identity. Seldom is it an issue of belief—belief in God or in the church. In one way or another, personally and professionally, they are struggling to maintain their integrity. Very few leave in bad faith.

A Sense of Mystery

If I search for a rational, reasonable explanation as to why I remain a priest, I find myself unsatisfied and frustrated. It's similar to a newly engaged person trying to explain why he or she has fallen in love with a certain individual and not another. This dimension of mystery is common to each of our lives. Do we not find that life's major decisions—whom we marry, the career we follow, the values we make our own—often transcend logic and reason?

The answer to the question is more poetry than prose, more intuitive than discursive. In the depths of my soul, I experienced a desire for communion with God that from the start (in my case, early childhood) was interwoven with a life of ministry as a priest. This desire indeed was mysterious. Whence did it come? Was it of the Spirit? Was it a divine invitation to priestly ministry? My years as a priest, almost 30 now, suggest that this desire was indeed of the Spirit.

Immediately this movement toward priesthood was in conflict with a powerful desire not unrelated to my desire for God: the desire for closeness to a young woman. I must confess that from the first day of school I wanted to be a priest and from that first day of school I was in love with a lovely and intriguing classmate. My affection for her endured through twelve years of education during which we shared the same homeroom. And my desire to be a priest endured and deepened. There is mystery here.

I am reminded of Edward Schillebeeckx's insight that speaks to the mystery of celibacy: it is simply "an inability to do otherwise." This inability to do otherwise has led me to discover that my truth is not only priestly ministry, but, paradoxically, celibate priestly ministry. In spite of the human longing for wife and family, for the joy and pain of a life shared intimately with another, I have discovered through the mercy of grace a communion of spirit with God and friends that remains unspeakable, that remains mystery. Always there were sustaining moments of communion. That's as close as I can come to an answer. These were feasts of grace and communion that happened for the most part at table. Certainly the Lord's table. I felt I was closest to the core of my truth when I was presiding and preaching at Eucharist.

Coaxed by the grace of God, individuals form an assembly, listen with a single ear to the living word, speak a prayer of sacrificial praise, eat and drink from the one table; and in so doing discover they are embraced by the divine presence, the divine mystery. No unbeliever can understand the profound privilege of participating in this feast of grace.

There are other feasts of grace that nourish and sustain me. These, too, are situated at table. Dinner with a dear friend or a married couple, with brother priests or with my family—all, at one time or another, have been sacraments of communion. On occasion, the warmth of God's eucharistic presence transforms a quiet restaurant table into sacred space. And "heart speaks to heart" (John Henry Newman).

A Question of Meaning

I cannot think of a more meaningful life than the life of a priest. I understand that this claim implies comparisons and evokes structures of hierarchy. That is not my intent. It is a personal confession of my own experience. For me, for this halting and often confused follower of the Christ, perseverance has been sustained by a profound sense of meaning and purpose. Depth psychologist C. G. Jung wisely observed that we humans cannot stand to live a meaningless life. And is not a major crisis of our age the awful meaningless that holds so many of us in a spirit-choking grip?

Here meaning and mystery embrace. The priest, as minister of God's word, is a messenger of meaning. It is his primary task to proclaim the paradox of the gospel: that life is to be found in dying to oneself; that freedom rests in our surrender to God's loving plan for us; that happiness follows upon selfless care and concern for our neighbor; that the first shall be last and the last first; that the least among us shall be the greatest! The priest knows in his heart, from his attempts to minister faithfully as a disciple of Christ and from his humbling witness to the grace of God reconciling broken spirits, that a life rich in meaning and grace flows inevitably from the gospel he is privileged to preach. In our confusion and heartache we cry, "Is there any word from the Lord?"

The priest answers with a resounding *Yes!* It is a word of deliverance and redemption. It is a word of ultimate meaning, for it is the Word made flesh.

A Sense of Mission

I remain a priest today quite simply because of the grace of God. But my task is to express how this grace grips me and sustains me. And this baring of my soul requires me to name that which I cannot name, the mystery of God's effusive Spirit loose in the world and loose in my soul. All I can say is that the mystery and meaning of my life as priest are intimately related to a sense of mission in which I am privileged to do my part in bringing to fulfillment the reign of God. In this sense, the priest, and every follower of Jesus Christ, is a hero. For the hero, as Joseph Campbell reminds us, is the individual who "has given his or her life to something bigger than oneself."

If there is a heroic dimension to the life of the priest, we priests know that along with the adventure of the mission there is the ordeal that awaits all who dare to follow the Christ, the ordeal that is at the heart of every heroic effort to live life in the spirit of the gospel. I have come to see that the ordeal required of discipleship is an integral part of the mystery. It leads to meaning and maturity, to humility and trust. In the midst of it all, I have come to understand that I have been sustained by the mercy of grace.

DONALD JETTE, S.S.S.

My answer to the question, Why am I a priest today? differs somewhat from the answer to the all-important question, Why did I become a priest? There is absolutely no doubt in my mind that I became a priest because God wanted me to be one. For a long time, I wondered why God chose me and not one or more of the other boys I grew up with. These young men, I know, had a lot more to give God and the church than I did. It took me a long time to believe that I was chosen because God loved me. God loved me enough to share his priesthood with me in a most intimate way.

The story of my vocation to the priesthood really began on the day of my first Communion, May 14, 1933. Before leaving the church, my mother and grandmother, who lived with us, took me aside and told me that after receiving communion my first words to Jesus should be "Please make me a priest someday." From that day on, both of them, as well as my aunt, who was a Sister of the Presentation, several of my teachers, and at least two of my parish priests constantly encouraged me to think of the priesthood.

In the eighth grade, a young nun, Sr. Agnes of Rome, fresh from Catholic University and destined for much higher things, became our teacher. I admired her. She knew I served Mass every day at the convent, something I did for several years. Out of the blue, one day she said to me: "Would you like me to teach you Latin? I know you are going to be a priest and this will help you when you go to the seminary."

The thought stuck in my mind that all these people were very good, and they evidently loved me. Consequently, what they were telling me to consider must be the best things that could ever happen to me. So, thanks to all these wonderful people, I entered the seminary at the age of 14, convinced that this was what God wanted, or all of these special people never would have been placed in my path.

I also believe that God wanted me to be a priest in the Congregation of the Blessed Sacrament. Long before I even heard of the Blessed Sacrament Community and of Peter Julian Eymard, I found myself attracted to prayer before the Blessed Sacrament.

I am sure that at ten or twelve years of age, my motives were far from perfect (I'm still having enough trouble in this regard), but during Forty Hours devotion, when the altar servers were asked to sign up for a half-hour at a time to insure that someone was always with the Blessed Sacrament, I found myself signing up for three or four half-hours. (Even my pious mother thought that was too much!) The sister in charge of the servers, Sr. Mary Clementine, noted that I had put my name in several spots and she asked me what I did during that time. Even though that was almost 60 years ago, I vividly remember my answer to her, and I marvel today at the grace this answer reveals: "I read the gospels in the Sunday Missal and try to realize that the same Jesus who worked these miracles, said those wonderful things, and helped so many people is the same Jesus who is in the host."

My journey to the priesthood was a relatively easy one. I knew what I wanted and never really looked back. And I was very happy during all these years. After ordination I taught in the major seminary for four years and then was sent to Manila, where I spent 14 glorious years in a downtown church. Santa Cruz, often working with the poorest of the poor.

My first real crisis came in the early 1970s when I was a pastor in New York City. Things were changing too fast for some, not fast enough for others, and I was caught in the middle. My ideals were slowly but surely drifting away, and I was very unhappy. Then, in the fall of 1974, I met a 23-year-old woman who was dying of leukemia. She was evidently God's messenger to me.

In the seven months I knew her, I can say that she, more than anyone else, made me take a second look at why I was a priest. I was struck one day when she said to me, "God has given you a true vocation to reveal his loving, compassionate heart to everyone you meet and talk to, as you have done for me. I am dying with no fear because you have convinced me how much God loves me."

I know that this is why I am a priest today. I have abundant opportunities to minister to people and help them feel God's love in a special way. In the past 42 years, I have had this privilege. I have celebrated about 18,000 Masses, preached to many hundreds of thousands of people. I have been at deathbeds, heard countless confessions, prepared several hundred couples for marriage, worked with what seems like a thousand committees, and baptized at least a couple of thousand babies. In short, I have had the opportunity to *be Christ* for others so many times, and I continue to have this chance in new and challenging ways every day.

I know I have often failed to represent God's love to others, but I can honestly say that over the past 20 years, at least, I have tried to do this every single day. I am truly happy that God called me to the priesthood and the religious life. I thank God every day for my vocation. I also ask God to keep using me, in spite of my weaknesses and failures, to bring his love, compassion, mercy, and forgiveness to the people who are sent my way.

JOSEPH McMAHON

W hy am I a priest today? I am a priest today because I believe that the Lord in his loving plan has called me to be one. Priesthood offers me the fullest opportunity to be myself, get in touch with my gifts, and to love others primarily through service.

Did I always want to be a priest when I was growing up? No. The Lord extended his call to me over a period of time through special people and experiences. The first people through whom the Lord spoke to me about my vocation were my parents. They were persons for whom faith and belief in the church were non-negotiables. For them, prayer and attendance at Eucharist were lifelines. I was also most fortunate in having a great pastor, who deeply loved the priesthood, the church, and all of us. It was said that if you wanted to give him a gift that he would keep, then you had to give him one that he could not give away.

It was in my senior year of high school that I first began to seriously think about being a priest. Our Catholic high school was a special place for me. We had youth ministry programs like Youth Leadership Workshop and Search for Christian Maturity that helped me experience that I was deeply loved and really had something to offer. There was also a priest, the spiritual director of our high school, whom I trusted and respected. At this time I began to talk to him, however hesitantly, about the possibility of becoming a priest.

At the conclusion of my senior year I decided to study for the priesthood, but this was not a final decision. I attended a college seminary for two years and then decided to leave even though it had been a positive experience for me. I completed my college education at a secular university and then worked for a year as a file clerk in a corporate law firm. It was there that one of the senior partners, a committed Catholic, said to me, "Joe, I think you would make a better priest than an attorney." After this, I returned to the seminary to study theology and was ordained to the diocesan priesthood in May 1984.

In contemplating priesthood my greatest fear was that I would not be happy. I knew that as a priest I would accomplish some good; I just feared I would not be happy. I can say in all honesty that this fear has not materialized. In fact, just the opposite has been the case. I believe that the priesthood offers me the fullest opportunity for happiness. I would characterize my experience of priesthood by borrowing the title of C. S. Lewis's spiritual autobiography, *Surprised by Joy.*

The opportunities for ministry that priesthood has afforded me are many. I have been given the gift of sharing people's lives at a deep level through parish ministry, youth ministry, vocation ministry, and now in my present assignment as Associate Principal at our diocesan high school. Each of these assignments has given me the precious invitation to share others' lives through leadership, prayer, the sacraments, counseling, and just being with them. Priesthood has led me to the truth that relationships are the most important gifts in life. Priesthood has also given me the broadest avenue to develop my relationships with the Lord and others.

What brings vitality to my priesthood? Spirituality. Priesthood offers me the best means to explore the spiritual dimension of life I consider basic. How do I do this? Through meditation on scripture, daily prayer, and Mass. I also draw life from making an annual directed retreat and meeting with my spiritual director on a regular basis. I am fortunate that I have had the same spiritual director since ordination; he is excellent for me. I also celebrate the sacrament of reconciliation regularly. These are the ways I tap into the spiritual realm of my life, keep my priesthood and my relationships with others alive.

Someone asked me recently if I believe there are persons who have a vocation to the priesthood but have not yet discovered it. I responded that I believe there are spiritually hungry persons, some of whom may well have a vocation to the priesthood. In order to connect with them we must be spiritually alive; being a priest gives me the fullest opportunity for this. Do I want to be a priest today? Yes, more than ever.

KEVIN C. SHEMUGA

I was sitting at my desk one cold and snowy Wednesday afternoon, trying to sift through the many telephone messages and a pile of paperwork when a telephone call came to our office. The woman had asked for a priest. I received the call and she said, "My father is dying. Will you please come to my parents' house?" My first reaction was frustration cloaked in a question to myself, "Why did I have to be the priest?" Then I told her I would be there in a half-hour.

I finished some work and left for the home. The wife of the dying man greeted me warmly at the door and led me to their bedroom. There I did indeed find a man on the doorstep of death. I anointed him and then sat by the bed with his wife. She told me that they had been married almost 50 years, years filled with joy and little sadness. He had been healthy his whole life until the past year. They loved each other, and their love, she said, would live on. She was not ready to let her husband go to God. Their daughter arrived as we talked, but then I had to get back to the parish.

As I was leaving, I leaned over the dying, unconscious man, and said, "Ernest, let God embrace you into life." His wife and daughter stood at the foot of the bed. To my amazement, Ernest raised his hands and I took them in my own. He nodded, and then looked at his wife and nodded again.

I went back to the parish and once again sat at my desk. The telephone call came 15 minutes later, from Ernest's wife. She told me that her husband had just died. She told him to let God embrace him. She was ready for that and she hoped he was ready for the Lord, and then he died.

The funeral Mass was one of great joy and hope. To this day, Ernest's wife still misses him, but it is a loss tempered by hope.

Why am I priest today? I am a priest for Ernest, his wife and daughter, and for all who need a priest at times of great joy and sorrow to share in their joy and pain. I am a priest to reveal the presence of Christ who came as servant of those who need comfort and hope.

In twelve years of priestly ministry, I have been privileged to preside and preach at the liturgy, to teach, and to lead people to God in love. This I have done in the name of Christ and the church. This was the commission given to me on the day of my ordination and prayed in the Preface of Priesthood:

> [Christ] appoints [priests] to renew in his name the sacrifice
> of our redemption as they set before your family his paschal
> meal. He calls them to lead your holy people in love, nour-
> ish them by your word, and strengthen them through the
> sacraments.

I am a priest today to work for justice in the church and in the world. Jesus' message was one of justice for the poor, the sinner, and for women. I am a priest today to move the church and the world to make the gospel message of justice a reality. I am a priest today for the outcast to show them a community that wants to include them in the circle of Christ's love.

For me, the ordained priesthood does not stand above or beyond the baptized. Priestly ministry is done in the midst of the baptized. This ministry is one of leadership, ordering the different gifts of the community, organizing ministry, and inviting the church to be a discipleship of equals. I am a priest today because I believe in Christ, the church, and that death is the entry into God's embrace.

If I am asked this question tomorrow, what will my answer be? My answer inevitably will change as I grow with the church. But one answer will remain constant: I am a priest today so that tomorrow someone will be sitting at a desk to take that urgent call.

WALTER J. BURGHARDT, S.J.

In February 1990, Mstislav Rostropovich, conductor of the National Symphony Orchestra in Washington, returned to Russia after 16 years of exile. He returned to give concerts, but even more importantly to heal—to begin healing political and personal wounds. Two decades ago, when Aleksandr Solzhenitsyn was harassed for his books on the Soviet Gulag, Rostropovich and his wife, Galina, took him into their home. "Slava" also composed a letter attacking the censors who had banned Solzhenitsyn's work. Before sending it, he was tormented.

> For 48 hours after I wrote that letter, Galina did not sleep but cried. She told me, "You have the right to destroy yourself, but what right do you have to destroy my life and the lives of your daughters?" But after 48 hours, Galina tells me, "Without this letter, you will not be able to continue living." We agreed to send it. I said, "They can't break us." But she was right. She said they would break us, and they did. Totally. (*Time,* February 26, 1990)

Exile in the United States meant dying and rising. "For me, at 47, life ended. I was born anew on May 26, 1974. There was no continuity. I was truly like a newborn. I couldn't speak the language of the place I was in. I had no place to live. I had no real friends." But with the Symphony a new career began. "This experience has made me emotionally twice as rich. I found a great deal more in music than I did when I lived in the Soviet Union. I re-examined everything, and I could see everything more vividly. All composers, even Beethoven, came to mean more."

Rostropovich opens my reflections because, in the twilight of my priestly existence, I have no time for bromides or placebos. These words are written in a period of priestly peril without parallel perhaps since the Reformation. I come with an uncommonly strong message, because it is only in the context of so challenging a charge that Christian confidence, hope, is possible in your lives. So then, three stages to my symphony: (1) crisis, (2) cross, (3) confidence.

Crisis

First, the crisis. No need to go into rich detail here, but a quick overview seems in order. What are some of the major elements that have fueled the contemporary crisis within our common priesthood?

1. *Celibacy.* Fifteen years ago, closing a profound article on "The Decision for Celibacy," Roger Balducelli wrote: "The questions that now come to occupy center stage are whether celibacy confers any recognizable strength to the [priest] as a person, any coherence and quality to his life, any effectiveness to his ministry and witness" (*Theological Studies,* 1975, p. 242).

For untold numbers of devoted priests, the answer is a decisive if agonizing no; theirs is a forced commitment that belies what should be a "gift of the Holy Spirit." In recent years celibacy has been made more complex by homosexuality—not only the acknowledged orientation of ever so many clergy, but the report (publicized by an author-priest known to many) that homosexual activity is quite common among priests, is rife in rectories, is muted by bishops as a lesser evil as long as the participants are discreet.

2. *Criticism.* In our immigrant church the priest was the "man for all seasons": the expert in all things from pulpit to politics. In mid-century priesthood was a noble profession, like medi-

cine and law; people tipped their hats to priests, as they tipped their hats when passing the parish church. Now our people are critical—seemingly more critical the more educated. Critical of us as celebrants and celibates, as theologians and preachers, as activists and administrators, as males. Priesthood is no longer something parents dream of for their firstborn. Who needs all this flak—and from people you spend your life serving? The antebellum slaves had it better.

3. *Crossfire.* Today priests more than any other ecclesial body are caught in crossfire. We are caught in the middle, in a no man's land: between liberal and conservative, between Vatican and laity, between bishop and parish. It is difficult for the nonknighted layperson to reach Rome with a land-based lay missile (unless the missile has the sins of a priest burned into its cone), hard for the ordinary Joe/Jane to pinpoint the whereabouts of the bishop. But priests make a clear, close, motionless target: at the altar, in the pulpit, in the rectory, by a postcard, local phone call, letter to the editor.

4. *Ineffectiveness.* Allied to criticism and crossfire is the suspicion that your priesthood has little influence on the lives of your people, that all too often your words are wasted on the wind. A certain amount of evidence cannot be denied: 80 percent of Catholic women consider artificial contraception legitimate; 30 percent of women who undergo abortions are Catholic; untold adults turn the homily off if one is brash enough to recommend an episcopal letter on peace or the economy; research shows that young people see in the church not so much an authority as at best a resource.

5. *Closures.* Parishes have been closed; schools have been closed. The result? Stress, disappointment, anger—especially among good priests personally affected. How not, when a priest's lifeblood has been poured into a school? How tolerate an adverse decision when you believe it makes no Christian sense, will hurt your people?

6. *Inadequate theology of priesthood.* I mean an undue emphasis on functions and roles. Too many define an ordained priest in terms of what he can *do* that an unordained person can *not* do. Here the crisis of identity has torn the guts of uncounted priests. They search for priesthood in terms of something specific to themselves, powers proper to priests, functions that distinguish them from laymen.

They do indeed discover such powers, such functions—what they alone can do: "This is my body." "I absolve you." But for all their significance, these functions take increasingly little of their time, so little of their lives. The rest of their existence—administration, schools, hospitals, preaching, spiritual direction—is lived in the suspicion that some man or woman in the pews could do it better.

7. *Burnout.* Fewer priests, greater obligations on those who remain, higher expectations from the laity, louder outcries when the expectations are not met. At the altar they expect you to be not a reverential robot, but a vibrant celebrant. In the pulpit they want a mind filled with God's revelation, a heart raptured by the Spirit, a tongue touched with hot coals. In human living they want you to be one with God *and* one with them, warmly human and still chaste; they challenge your pretensions to poverty; they demand that you feed their faith *and* struggle for justice.

In consequence, less if any privacy; less time to pray, to contemplate; less time for relaxation, for a "break"; less time to prepare homilies; less time to "fill the cup."

8. *Fear.* Before Vatican II, the priesthood may not have been paradise, but it was studded with stability and security. You could commit yourself with confidence to a celibate existence for life, be respected for it by a people who rarely questioned it, and expect to die serenely in the warm arms of a Christ you had served as your one Master. Now we even share lay insecurities:

how to find and keep a job, how to retire without bitterness, how to survive old age, how to die believing, hoping, loving.

9. *Aging.* A recent letter to me from a priest in an eastern diocese reads in Part:

> I remember reading, toward the end of your *Seasons That Laugh or Weep,* about integration vs. despair. I would like you to speak to our priests about their experience of living in middle adulthood and old age without bitterness or resentment. Aging seems for some a real enemy and not an experience of grace. I would like to invite the majority of our priests over 55 and, in fact, dedicate your presentation to them. Very little is being done for our older men, except for a beautiful retirement facility and the usual physical care piece. I would like you to address the spiritual parts of aging with grace. I realize it is a big task and I would be grateful if you would share your experiences with my brothers.

Cross

So much for crisis. I have not come to you with a hatful of answers. The nine crises I have sketched, and others more familiar to you than to me, call for continuing dialogue with church leaders and bishops, men like Cardinal Bernardin who in 1982 claimed that priests "are called to be challengers, enablers, life-givers, poets of life, music makers, dreamers of dreams." I want to confront you not with pat solutions but with a radical risk.

I begin by submitting that the pattern, the prototype, of your priestly service is the Christ Paul pictured in the hymn he quoted to the Christians of Philippi when he urged them to have the mind-set of Christ,

> who, though his condition was divine,
> did not consider equality with God
> something to exploit for selfish gain,
> but emptied himself,

taking on the condition of a slave,
becoming like human beings.
And being found in human form,
he humbled himself still further
with an obedience that meant death,
even death on a cross. (Phil 2:6-8)

In that context, recall a remarkable sentence from the later works of Karl Rahner: "According to scripture we may safely say that Jesus in his life was the *believer*...and that he was consequently the one who hopes absolutely and in regard to God and men the one who loves absolutely" ("Following the Crucified," *Theological Investigations 18: God and Revelation.* New York: Crossroad, 1983, p. 165).

Basic to the human life of Jesus was a God-given gift we often overlook: Jesus had to live by a wedding of faith and hope. For all that he was God, his whole human existence called for confident trust in the love of his Father. He was as genuinely human as you and I.

Luke tells us he grew not only in size but "in wisdom" (Lk 2:52). He not only tired; he wept—over Jerusalem and Lazarus, over his city and his friend. Relatives were concerned not simply for his safety but for his sanity; some thought him quite mad. There were towns where "he could do no mighty work...because of their unbelief" (Mk 6:5-6). His fellow Nazareans, angered at his preaching, tried to toss him over a cliff. When he cast out devils, the Pharisees claimed he did so "through the prince of devils" (Mt 12:24). He offered his flesh to eat, his blood to drink, and "many of his disciples drew back and no longer went about with him" (Jn 6:66). Time and again he beat his fists in frustration against the pride of his people, their smallness and stubbornness, their rejection of him and his words. Against perverse, pigheaded unbelief he was helpless. All he could do was trust in his Father.

The cross over Jesus' life came to a climax on Calvary. Here Rahner has a packed and poignant paragraph. It is not bedtime reading, but for insight into Jesus it is worth every bead of intellectual and spiritual sweat you can summon up.

> In the unity of [his] faith, hope, and love, Jesus surrendered himself in his death unconditionally to the absolute mystery that he called his Father, into whose hands he committed his existence, when in the night of death and God-forsakenness he was deprived of everything that is otherwise regarded as the content of a human existence: life, honour, acceptance in earthly and religious fellowship, and so on—Everything fell away from him, even the perceptible security of the closeness of God's love, and in this trackless dark there prevailed silently only the mystery that in itself and it its freedom has no name and to which he nevertheless calmly surrendered himself as to eternal love and not to the hell of futility…He who came out of God's glory did not merely descend into our human life, but also fell into the abyss of our death, and his dying began when he began to live and came to an end on the cross when he bowed his head and died. (ibid., pp. 165–66)

And sear this into your Christology: For all that he was God, this man, like us, died not with experience of resurrection but with faith in his Father; he died not with unassailable proof of resurrection but with hope of life for ever.

And what of you? For these agonizing years I commend to you an intense focus of Rahner's last years: what he called "the cross…erected over history." For Calvary did not write finis to crucifixion; it was the prelude to St. Paul's "in my flesh I complete what is lacking in Christ's afflictions for the sake of his body, that is, the church, of which I became a minister according to the divine office which was given to me for you, to make the word of God fully known" (Col 1:24–25).

In the context of the current crisis, I suggest that your service as priests will be most Christian, most effective, ultimately most gratifying personallly if you follow the Crucified. To make sense of this, several observations.

First, the very word "follow." It is not simply synonymous with "imitate." "Imitate" has indeed precious precedent in Paul: "Be imitators of me, as I am of Christ" (1 Cor 11:1). Still, as Rahner saw so clearly,

> we are not really expected to copy and reproduce the life of Jesus as such. We live in historical situations different from those in which Jesus himself lived, we have a different and always unique task which is not the same as that which confronted him in his own historically conditioned and restricted existence; he and we together form the one Christ of the one and unique total history of salvation, in which, for all our crucial dependence on him and on his historical existence in life and death, we do not reproduce him, but (as Paul says) complete his historical individual reality (ibid., p. 158)

Very simply, in the lives of all graced men and women there are realizations of faith, hope, and love which in his restricted existence Jesus did not and could not experience. He was a man, not a woman; he was a teacher, but not a scholar; he did not experience old age or Alzheimer's disease; he did not even live to be a Jesuit!

More accurate, then, than "imitate" is "follow," be Jesus' disciple. And if you ask where concretely, for any and every Christian, independently of time and circumstance, Christ is to be followed, we must answer with Rahner: "the Christian, every Christian at all times, follows Jesus by *dying* with him; following Jesus has its ultimate truth and reality and universality in the following of the Crucified…" (ibid., pp. 160–61).

Second, following the Crucified, following Jesus in our dying, is not limited to the close of our earth-bound existence, to the terminal cancer, the cardiac arrest. Dying in a theological sense begins when living begins; we share in Jesus' dying by sharing in his cross through the whole of our lives. Not only physical pain—sinusitis, ileitis, hemorrhoids—but the agonies that are rather psychological and spiritual. I mean, concretely, the agonies that nail you to your priestly crosses today: celibacy, criticism, crossfire, ineffectiveness, closures, burnout, fear, aging.

In these and other instances of what Rahner called "dying in installments," we confront the question of how to cope. How do I cope? Do I just protest? Do I sulk? Do I nurse my grievances? Do I despair? Do I cling all the more desperately to what has not been taken from me? Or do I try to put my passion in touch with Christ's, "complete what is lacking in Christ's afflictions for the sake of his body, the church"? Do I see such "breakdowns" as what Rahner terms "events of grace"?

I am not prodding you into passivity: "Pile it on, Lord!" Nor am I speaking from an ivory tower. In my middle years there was bitter anguish—from bouts with hypochondria and sinfulness, through the sudden deaths of my dearest friends Gustave Weigel and John Courtney Murray and the lingering psychic dying of my mother, to the traumatic death of the Woodstock Theological Seminary that had housed my head and my heart till I neared sixty.

Ignatius Loyola, on his own admission, could have accepted in 15 minutes the destruction of his life-work, the Society of Jesus. It took me five or six years to come to terms with Woodstock's closing, to transcend the natural resentments, to fling away those unanswerable questionings about right and wrong, wisdom or folly, to focus in my heart what I was preaching with my lips: only Jesus is indispensable, Jesus alone is irreplaceable. "In no other name is there salvation save in the name of Jesus" (Acts 4:12).

Third, following the Crucified may demand that you rethink, refine, redefine what a down-to-earth Christian spirituality involves. In by-gone days "Christian spirituality was conceived as an ascent to a height of what was called 'Christian perfection,' with the ways and stages of this ascent...outlined and marked out in advance by the theology of the spiritual life" (Karl Rahner, "The Spirituality of the Priest in the Light of His Office," *Theological Investigations* 19: *Faith and Ministry.* New York: Crossroad, 1983, pp. 133–34).

Today the more experienced among suffering servants are less likely to see the spiritual life as a master plan for steady progress. It makes more sense, theological and spiritual, to see myself "as someone who is led by God's providence in [my] life history through continually new and surprising situations, in which [I] can never say from the outset what will happen and how [I] must cope with it" (ibid., p. 134). Genuine discipleship is more a matter of faithful following, not ever onwards and upwards, rather with the courage to expect the unexpected, to respond to the unexpected not from 3x5 file cards but in total openness to a Spirit who, like Augustine's Beauty, is ever ancient, ever new.

It is then that the spiritual life becomes not a fearful scaling of icy slopes with supernal crampons and axes, but a glorious adventure in which you and I can predict only two things with confidence: (1) the Spirit will ceaselessly surprise us and (2) however unexpected the event, God will be there.

Fourth, such following of the Crucified renders your ministry at once less difficult and more difficult. Less difficult because you do not come to your sisters and brothers primarily with an articulate theology, with answers to all problems. You come as you are, aware of your own brokenness, conscious that you are *wounded* healers, far more effective with "the foolishness...and the weakness of God" (1 Cor 1:25) than with your own wisdom and strength.

More difficult because you must let your people see you as the people of Palestine saw Jesus: not in the glory you have with the Father, but in your self-emptying, in your "form of a slave," in your "obedience that [means] death, even death on a cross."

Confidence

Paradoxically, death on a cross leads directly into my third point: confidence. The only genuinely Christian counter-pole to the dying involved in celibacy and burnout, in criticism and closures, in fear and aging, is heralded in the mind-shivering paschal proclamation from the First Epistle of Peter:

> Blessed be the God and Father of our Lord Jesus Christ! By his great mercy we have been born anew to a living hope through the resurrection of Jesus Christ from the dead, and to an inheritance which is imperishable, undefiled, and unfading, kept in heaven for you, who by God's power are guarded through faith for a salvation ready to be revealed in the last time. In this you rejoice, though now for a little while you may have to suffer various trials, so that the genuineness of your faith, more precious than gold which though perishable is tested by fire, may redound to praise and glory and honor at the revelation of Jesus Christ. Without having seen him you love him; though you do not now see him you believe in him and rejoice with unutterable and exalted joy, obtaining as the outcome of your faith the salvation of your souls. (1:3–9)

This is not a passage you simply preach to your people. This is *your* good news. Here is the heart of the Christian mystery: "By [God's] great mercy we have been born anew to a living hope through the resurrection of Jesus Christ from the dead." It begins with resurrection.

St. Paul put it pungently: "If Christ has not been raised, your faith is futile and you are still in your sins" (1 Cor 15:17). Make no mistake! If Jesus did not really come back to life, forget it! Go home, turn on the Movie Channel, revel in violence or sex or whatever turns you on. But don't waste your time on a Christ who merely lives in our memories, simply in our hearts, only in a picture frame. That Christ deserves to stay dead.

No, our Christ is alive. Alive now. More alive than you and I have ever been. Alive in his Godhead and in the humanity God's Son borrowed from us for ever. Alive for us, for you and me; alive for what the Letter of Peter calls a rebirth.

What does it mean to be "born anew"? Basically, it means you have a new life. You know what it means, what it feels like, to be humanly alive. You can think, shape an idea, argue a point, listen to Mozart or Michael Jackson. You can do things. I mean, you can work and play, walk and sing, love and laugh, "pump iron" or sway to aerobics.

Something similar happens when you are gifted with new life in Christ. You can believe what passes proof. I mean, you can take God's word for it that God loves you and lives in you, that God died for you and rose for you, that life does not end at 40 or 90, that death is a prelude to life without end.

And you can do things not possible unless Christ had died and risen for you. You can love God more intensely than man ever loved woman, love your sisters and brothers as Jesus himself loves them. Take Jesus' word for it: "If you have faith as small as a grain of mustard seed, you will say to this mountain, 'Move hence to yonder place,' and it will move; and nothing will be impossible to you" (Mt 17:20).

Briefly, in that extraordinary sentence from the First Epistle of Peter, "Without having seen [Jesus] you love him; though you do not now see him you believe in him" (1 Pt 1:8). This is what it means to be alive in Christ. But the same letter trumpets not only faith and love; it claims "we have been born anew to a living hope" (v. 3).

Not an Anglo-Saxon "stiff upper lip, old boy." No. Christian hope is a gift of God. Not wishful thinking: I hope Israel and the PLO can come to peaceful terms; I hope the decision to prune parish expenditures will disappear into thin air; I hope I can prepare a good sermon on the way from rectory to church.

Christian hope is confident expectation—confidence that a God who is ceaselessly faithful despite my infidelities will always be there for me, will be there for me in the hereafter.

Such is the hope that marks a follower of Christ. Such is the hope that marked the earthly Jesus—a Jesus who was afraid, did not want to die, begged his Father in the garden of agony to take this cup from him: "Father, don't let me die!" Still, "not my will but thine be done" (Lk 22:42). And an angel came from his

Father, gave him strength to carry his cross to Calvary, strength to murmur with parched lips to a Father who seemed to have forsaken him, "Into your hands I entrust my spirit" (Lk 23:46). Such is the hope that left Calvary's tomb empty.

Now this is not some pietistic spirituality; it is the only Christian counterpoise to the fears that afflict you and me. Begin with the First Letter of John: "There is no fear in love, but perfect love casts out fear" (4:18). It's a fact: perfect love can destroy all fear.

You see it all through Christian history—from the original apostles leaving the threatening council "rejoicing that they were counted worthy to suffer dishonor for the name" (Acts 5:41), through Joan of Arc at the stake and Thomas More on the scaffold, to Mother Teresa and her 3000 Missionaries of Charity touching plague and AIDS with love. They are men and women who are afraid of nothing. Not that they are masochists, take pleasure in pain. Pain hurts them as much as it hurts us. But unreserved love enables them to put into practice the promise of Paul, "God is faithful...will not let you be tried beyond your strength, but with the trial will also [enable you] to endure it" (1 Cor 10:13).

But I suspect that most Christians, perhaps most of you, are not able to destroy all fear, all anxiety, all anger, all resentment. These emotions are instinctive, nestle in our bones, strike when we least expect them. What then? Hope; Christian hope. With hope, you can cope, cope with fear, cope with the fear and dread, the anxiety and indignation, the discouragement and near despair.

One personal example. Let me be uncommonly honest. I am not running toward death with open arms; in fact, I'm dragging my feet. I cannot yet bring myself to echo St. Paul, "My desire is to depart [to die] and to be with Christ" (Phil 1:23). Why? Several reasons.

I've never been a friend of pain; I fear a lingering illness; I am morbidly mindful of my mother's six years in a nursing home—six years without memory, without mind. And I love this life so passionately that I resonate to poet Francis Thompson's "Hound of Heaven":

> ...though I knew His love who followed,
>   Yet was I sore adread
> Lest, having Him, I must have naught beside.

Still, of one thing I am confident, that when illness and dying do strike, God will be there: a Father who is especially then a Mother, a Christ who rose from the rock for my resurrection, a Holy Spirit whose other name is Love.

As for you, the paschal mystery, the resurrection of Jesus, trumpets an incredibly consoling truth. Whoever you are, whatever your pain or problem, anxiety or affliction, frustration or failure, you need never despair. Not that pain will be converted into pleasure, disappointment into delight, problems conveniently solved, failure turned to instant success. Simply that the promise of Jesus can come true: "So you have sorrow now, but I will see you again and your hearts will rejoice, and your joy no one will take from you" (Jn 16:22).

I say the promise of Jesus *can* come true. For living hope is not something automatic: press H on your computer and out comes Christian hope. Hope was indeed infused in you when baptismal waters bathed your brow. But that gift has to grow, has to be nurtured like a delicate flower. And it grows best if your relationship to Jesus is the prayer lyricized in the musical *Godspell:* "This, Lord, I pray: to see you more clearly, love your more dearly, follow you more nearly." It is less than Christian to treat Christ only as a God of foxholes, a Savior of missions impossible, someone you can call on when living gets desperate, when human help is helpless—when the bishop has shut his ears to both reason and revelation.

The God of your hope is deep inside you, closer to you than you are to yourself. To live with living hope is to live lovingly with the source of hope, the Jesus who dies and rose precisely to give you hope.

In sum, my brothers in our one High Priest, I am simply stressing what is surely known to you intellectually but may not have gotten into your Christian guts. The hope we need to face up to our most profound fears and frustrations is not in the power of man or woman to provide. I am not defaming the psychiatrist's couch or the philosopher's portico; these have proven their human value, can even help us become more Christian. But in the last analysis the hope you and I need to live like Christ is a gift of God, a gift that is actually part of our Christian make-up, a gift we paradoxical priests all too often leave untapped, allow to rust.

The only reliable remedy I know for such rusting is an injection of love. Get closer to Christ; rest, like the Beloved Disciple at the Last Supper, "close to the breast of Jesus" (Jn 13:23); humbly place in his hands your specific helplessness, your experience of hopelessness. Get closer to this earth's images of Christ, especially the hopelessly crucified; touch one of them in selfless love.

Let me end where I began: with Slava Rostropovich. "For me, at 47, life ended. I was born anew on May 26, 1974. There was no continuity. I was truly like a newborn. I couldn't speak the language of the place I was in. I had no place to live. I had no real friends."

His rebirth in the States is my prayer for you. May your experience of fear or frustration, of anxiety or resentment, of desolation or despair make you "emotionally twice as rich." May you find "a great deal more in [your priestly] music" than you ever did before. Re-examining everything, may all you do from now on, everything you experience, come to "mean more," have a depth of meaning untapped before. In brief, may you too be reborn into a living hope. A...living...hope.

ABOUT THE CONTRIBUTORS

Anthony M. Pilla, Bishop of Cleveland, has also served as President of the National Council of Catholic Bishops.

George G. Higgins, originally of Chicago, has long been the foremost Catholic spokesman in the American labor movement and is also a syndicated columnist on social issues.

Frank J. McNulty, of the Archdiocese of Newark, has been an author, retreat leader, pastor, and a leader among American diocesan priests.

Joseph M. Champlin, of the Diocese of Syracuse, is a well-known author on liturgical and pastoral topics.

Walter M. Bunofsky, S.V.D., is a writer and teacher from the Divine Word College in Iowa.

James E. Sheil is a U.S. Army chaplain and has served in pastoral positions in Germany. He is from the Diocese of Cleveland.

Wilton D. Gregory, Bishop of Belleville, Illinois, has written extensively on liturgy and theological developments.

Philip M. Cioppa, of the Diocese of Albany, New York, has been the Director of the Northwest Office for Hispanic Affairs in Yakima, Washington.

Charles J. Ritty, of the Diocese of Cleveland, has served in many pastoral and diocesan ministries in more than 50 years of priestly service.

Ralph J. Friedrich, of the Diocese of Youngstown, Ohio, has also served for many years as a missionary in El Salvador.

Francis D. Costa, S.S.S., has been Provincial of the Congregation of the Blessed Sacrament as well as a pastor and seminary professor.

Michael J. Hunt, C.S.P., of the Paulist Fathers, has served as a chaplain at secular universities and is currently an associate editor at Paulist Press.

Sylvester D. Ryan, Bishop of Monterey, California, has also served as a teacher, administrator, and pastor.

John Gartner, S.S.S., of the Congregation of the Blessed Sacrament, has served in parish ministry in New Mexico.

John Peter Singler, a priest of Cleveland, has served on a pastoral team in Willowick, Ohio.

Robert F. Morneau, Auxiliary Bishop of Green Bay, Wisconsin, has written and lectured widely on prayer and spirituality.

Anthony Schueller, S.S.S., has been Vicar Provincial of the Congregation of the Blessed Sacrament and an editor of *Emmanuel* magazine.

J. G. Hanley edited the *Canadian Register*, a chain of Catholic newspapers in his native Canada for nearly 30 years.

Frederico J. G. Ablog, S.S.S., a native of the Philippines, has been involved in pastoral work in Highland Heights, Ohio.

James McCullough, has taught for many years at Gannon University in Erie, Pennsylvania.

John MacInnis has been Spiritual Director at St. John's Seminary in Boston and also served in the Catholic campus ministry at Harvard University.

Eugene LaVerdiere, S.S.S., is a widely known writer and speaker and has served as editor of *Emmanuel* magazine. He is a member of the Congregation of the Blessed Sacrament.

Thomas J. Morgan, of the Diocese of Camden, has served as a pastor in Pennsville, New Jersey.

Richard Bell, M.M., a member of Maryknoll, has served as a pastor in Taiwan.

Walter A. Riendeau, S.S.S., of the Congregation of the Blessed Sacrament, is a canon lawyer and seminary professor who has also served as a pastor in Utah.

Donald B. Cozzens has served as the Vicar for Clergy and Religious in the Diocese of Cleveland, in addition to extensive writing and publications on the priestly life.

Donald Jette, S.S.S., has served in the Philippines, New York, and Maine. He has also been the Provincial Superior of the Congregation of the Blessed Sacrament.

Joseph McMahon teaches at Father Ryan High School in Nashville, Tennessee.

Kevin C. Shemuga has served in parish ministry in the Diocese of Cleveland.

Walter J. Burghardt, S.J., is a well-known Jesuit theologian and preacher. He is the former editor of *Theological Studies* and has written many books on preaching and liturgy. His contribution to this collection is an address he gave to the priest-jubilarians of the Archdiocese of Chicago on May 9, 1990.